Cheshire Walks
with Children

Nick Lambert

First edition printed 1996
Reprinted 2003, 2005

Second edition printed 2009

Published by Sigma Leisure – an imprint of
Sigma Press, Stobart House, Pontyclerc, Penybanc Road
Ammanford, Carmarthenshire SA18 3HP
This edition has been completely revised and updated with new maps and photographs

British Library Cataloguing in Publication Data

A CIP record for this book is available from the British Library

ISBN: 978-1-85058-874-0

Typesetting and Design by: Sigma Press, Ammanford, Carms

Maps: Nick Lambert

Photographs: Nick Lambert

Printed by: Cromwell Press Group, Trowbrige, Wiltshire

Disclaimer: The information in this book is given in good faith and is believed to be correct at the time of publication. Care should always be taken when walking in hill country. Where appropriate, attention has been drawn to matters of safety. The author and publisher cannot take responsibility for any accidents or injury incurred whilst following these walks. Only you can judge your own fitness, competence and experience. Do not rely solely on sketch maps for navigation: we strongly recommend the use of appropriate Ordnance Survey (or equivalent) maps.

Preface

At the time of writing Britain is in the grip of the so-called Credit Crunch. There are many pressures in our society, and I think the need to take time out and relax is even greater than ever. On the bright side walking is free! Walking reduces tension, promotes fitness and releases feel-good endorphins. Get your boots on and get out there!

Many of the walks in this book are probably only a short journey from your home. I hope they enable you to have fun family days out; I hope they encourage a new generation of walkers and sow a seed in the young that we need to cherish our countryside and our environment and make the most of what we have left.

I have really enjoyed re-walking all these routes again for the new revised and updated version of this book. Some of the walks – mainly those in north Cheshire, I know and walk regularly; others, mainly in the "deep south", I haven't managed to re-walk since the planning of the original book, over twelve years ago. There were many small changes and there were a couple of big changes – the biggest being at Delamere Forest, where half of my original walk is now underwater, as the Forestry Commission have flooded an area of the forest to create a wetland environment.

Cheshire is a beautiful county – walk it and enjoy it, try not to disturb or disrupt it, walk it safely and responsibly and come back again to enjoy it another day.

Nick Lambert
November 2009

Preface To First Edition

Cheshire, with its vast plain and its gentle hills, makes ideal walking country for children. I have walked its network of footpaths and quiet bridleways many times with my family, and on numerous occasions have enjoyed spectacular days alone. I hope walking in Cheshire provides you and your family with as much pleasure it has given me and mine.

All route directions have been checked and double checked, but places change. Houses are sold and sometimes alter their names.

Trees are cut down, footpaths are re-routed and a stile can be replaced by a gate etc etc. The route maps are only intended as a rough guide to the walk. Please carry the appropriate Ordnance Survey map with you to help you in case you get lost, though hopefully that won't be necessary.

And finally ... many of the walks pass meres and rivers where there are many ducks and water birds, so take some bread along; children love feeding ducks, but ducks these days are a health-conscious species and apparently, they prefer brown bread, as white bread interferes with their digestive system. So next time you're out shopping, pop a wholemeal loaf in your basket for those fibre-enlightened wildfowl.

Contents

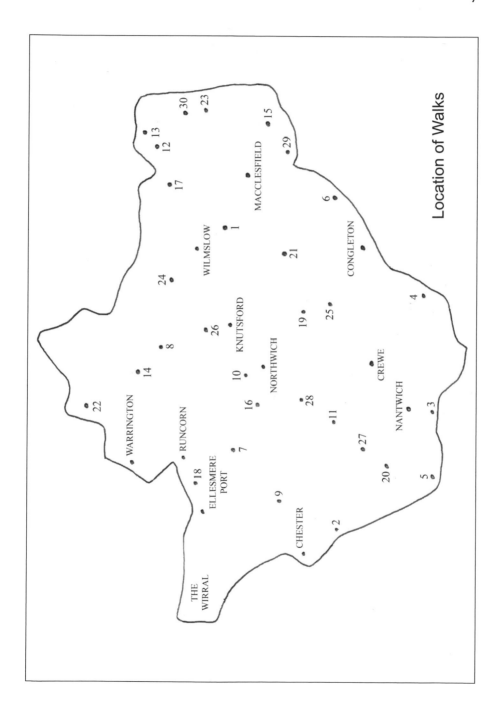

Location of Walks

The Country Code
(and some other commonsense advice)

First And Foremost...

- Please ensure you wear appropriate footwear for your walk

- Please ensure you have an appropriate map with you, as foot paths and rights of way occasionally change

- Just in case ... it's always a good idea to take your mobile phone in case of emergencies, and make sure someone at home knows where you've gone and when to expect you back

The Country Code...

- Don't drop litter. If there is no bin, take it home with you

- The countryside should be a place of peace and tranquillity. Do not ruin it for other people

- Close all gates after you, otherwise you might cause flocks of sheep to stray onto the road and get run over

- Keep dogs on leads when there are farm animals around, and keep them under close control at all times

- Do not try to get too near to wild animals, as many of them will be frightened and may BITE!

- If stroking farm animals such as horses, keep fingers WELL AWAY from their mouths, or you may lose them

- Always stick to the public footpaths/bridleways, and do not stray onto private land

- Some farms use electric fences to separate fields. These are usually a single wire held up by occasional plastic supports. The charge is only low, and won't kill you. Even so, it's not a good idea to grab hold of them, as a shock can be alarming

- Do not cross railway lines, except by proper crossing places, such as bridges

- Always walk on the right hand side of a lane or road, so that you are walking TOWARDS the traffic, so that you can see any approaching vehicle.Keep well into the side of the road and keep in single file. Restrain small children as traffic approaches

- Do not pick wild flowers. Leave them for others to enjoy

- Never eat wild berries. They may look colourful and tasty, like sweets, but many are deadly poisonous. The same goes for mushrooms and toadstools. No matter how nice and colourful they look, don't touch them

- Never fool around near water. Do not paddle in a stream or pond unless an adult says it is safe to do so

- Respect the countryside and enjoy your walk!

A Note About Public Rights Of Way

Countryside in any county can change, with different crops grown in fields each year. If the footpath across a farmed field is lost under a crop of wheat, corn etc, then you have the right to make your way through that crop and you have the legal right to trespass, where necessary, in order to by-pass any illegal obstacle, but take care not to damage any crop or property.

  Public Footpaths are in many cases ancient rights of way, and not even the landowner has the right to prevent their use. If you encounter hazards or blocked paths on your walk, then the Ramblers' Association would like to hear from you, but first, always double check the correct route of the right of way on an up-to-date Ordnance Survey map.

  The Ramblers' Association
  1/5 Wandsworth Road
  London
  SW8 2XX

Public Transport Information

Cheshire Traveline

For bus and rail information within the county, and getting into the county: 0871 200 22 33

For internet rail enquiries visit www.nationalrail.co.uk

For internet details about Cheshire buses visit Cheshire County Council's Bus Homepage at www.cheshire.gov.uk and click on buses

Introductory notes on the text

Directions are numbered and appear in **bold**, so they can be seen at a glance.

Other information for parents appears in *italics*.

 Information in this type is for the children, to be read aloud to them, or for them to read themselves, depending on their age and abilities.

Checklists appear at the end of each walk, for the child to tick off things as they see them. If you do not want to write in the book, copy out the checklist on a piece of paper, and give one to each child, so they can compete to see who spots the most.

The maps are intended only as a rough guide to the route and are not drawn to scale. Unless otherwise stated north is upwards. Only buildings important to the route are shown.

The index chart allows you to plan your day at a glance, to check each route has the features or facilities you require. For more information on these see the individual route.

Index Chart

The index chart allows you to plan your day at a glance, to check each route has the features or facilities you require. For more information on these see the individual route.

	RAIL	BUS	CAFE	PUBS	WET WEATHER	FLAT	HISTORICAL	PUSH CHAIRS	SPECIAL FEATURES
1 ALDERLEY	*	*	*	*			various	*	legends, caves
2 ALDFORD		*		*		*	estate village	*	
3 AUDLEM		*	*	*		*		*	canals and locks
4 BARTHOMLEY		*		*		*	fighting in civil war		
5 BIG MERE				*			wildfowl		
6 THE CLOUD							stone age burial chamber		
7 DELAMERE	*	*	*	*	*	*		**	Go Ape! Cycle hire
8 DUNHAM MASSEY		*	*	*		*	stately home	**	deer
9 GREAT BARROW		*		*		*		*	
10 GREAT BUDWORTH		*	*	*		*	estate village & hall		
11 LITTLE BUDWORTH		*	*	*		*		*	heathland wildlife
12 LYME/BOWSTONES	*	*	*	*			stately home		deer, playground, ducks
13 LYME PARK/DISLEY	*	*	*	*			stately home		deer, playground, ducks
14 LYMM DAM		*		*		*		**	wildfowl
15 MACFLD FOREST		*	*						views
16 MARBURY	*	*				*		**	bird hide
17 MIDDLEWOOD	*	*	*	*		*		*	
18 OVER PEOVER				*		*	stately home		

	RAIL	BUS	CAFE	PUBS	WET WEATHER	FLAT	HISTORICAL	PUSH CHAIRS	SPECIAL FEATURES
19 OVERTON HILL				*					estuary views
20 PECKFORTON		*	*	*	*		two castles		candle factory
21 REDESMERE		*				*	stately home		wildfowl
22 RISLEY MOSS	*				*	*		**	hides visitor centre
23 SHINING TOR									superb views
24 STYAL WOODS	*	*	*	*			cotton mill, old village	*	mill/museum
25 SWETTENHAM			*	*					nature reserve
26 TATTON PARK	*	*	*	*	*	*	two halls	**	deer, playground, lake bathing
27 WHARTON'S LOCK				*		*		*	canal and lock
28 WHITEGATE WAY	*			*			old railway & station	*	
29 WINCLE				*					
30 WINDGATHER							Pym Chair		rock climbing

Notes and Key

Rail: * Routes that are within a short walk of a railway station

Bus: * Routes that are within a short walk from a bus stop

Cafe: * A cafe or tearoom along the route or within easy walking distance

Pubs: * A pub along the route where families are welcome, with seats outside or a family room

Wet Weather: * Walks suitable for bad weather/winter, usually with gravelled paths or all-weather surfaces

Flat: * The route is more or less flat, or can be made flat using escape routes

Historical: * A place of historical interest features along the route, or close by

Pushchairs: * Walks with at least a small route suitable for pushchairs, though it may involve some effort
** Complete circular routes that are totally suitable, or can be made suitable for pushchairs

Special features: * Places of specific interest to children along the route or close by

1. Alderley Edge

Alderley Edge is a popular spot for Sunday walks and days out. In summer it can get very busy in the car parks and on the main paths, but there are still areas where you can walk in peace and might not meet a soul, such as Clockhouse Wood on the eastern fringes. Alderley is a mysterious place with more than its fair share of tales about witches, wizards, goblins and things that go bump in the night. The Edge and surrounding area provided an eerie setting for Alan Garner's epic tales 'The Weirdstone of Brazinghamen' and 'The Moon of Gomrath'. Garner's family lived for generations in a cottage at the foot of the Edge and he chronicles their story in 'The Stone Book Quartet'.

Alderley was once the site of much mining activity. The dangerous

Starting point	**Main car park (SJ860773) off Macclesfield Road (B5087) between Macclesfield and Alderley Edge village**
By rail	**Alderley Edge station. Walk through the village to the roundabout and take Macclesfield Road uphill to the Edge**
Distance	**Entire route – 3 miles** **Pushchair route about 1 mile**
Terrain	**Good gravelled paths at the top of the Edge. Winding paths at the bottom of the Edge, prone to muddiness in wet weather**
Maps	**OS Explorer 268 or Landranger 118**
Public toilets	**Main car park**
Refreshments	**Wizard Tea Room, near to main car park. Open only at weekends. Other places in Alderley village**
Pushchairs	**Short pushchair route. Begin with Direction 1**

mines are now all sealed and the Edge is under the guardianship of the National Trust.

1. **From the main car park follow the pathway towards the Wizard Tea Rooms. (On entering the car park it is on the left – often there is a Tational Trust information stand here.)**

☺ The Wizard Tea Room was once an old barn; it is built of rough stone which has been painted white. At the side you can see an old stable door. The top part could be opened so horses could see out. Above is a door to the loft, where hay would have been kept, which the animals could eat in winter.

   Next to the tea room is a National Trust Information Room with information about the caves and history of the Edge.

2. **From the Tea Room continue along the driveway towards the woods. Bear left before the warden's house, following the path between the trees.**

3. **Keep to the main path straight ahead.**

☺ Over 250 years ago there were no trees at Alderley Edge; it was just bare rock, heather and low bushes. But then Lord Stanley, who owned much of the lands around Alderley, planted Scots Pines on the highest points of the Edge, and some years later birch were planted, at which point the Edge was fenced off and became private. On certain days of the year the local villagers were allowed to visit the woods for a day out.

4. **Continue ahead, passing a fenced grassy area on your right.**

   At the fenced grassy area: indicate the rocky fault line to the right which is Engine Vein Mine.

☺ This is a mine, which at one time was worked for copper. It is thought that mining may have taken place at Alderley as early as Roman times, but it has certainly gone on for several hundred years, though there is no mining here now.
   There are no natural caves at Alderley at all. All the tunnels

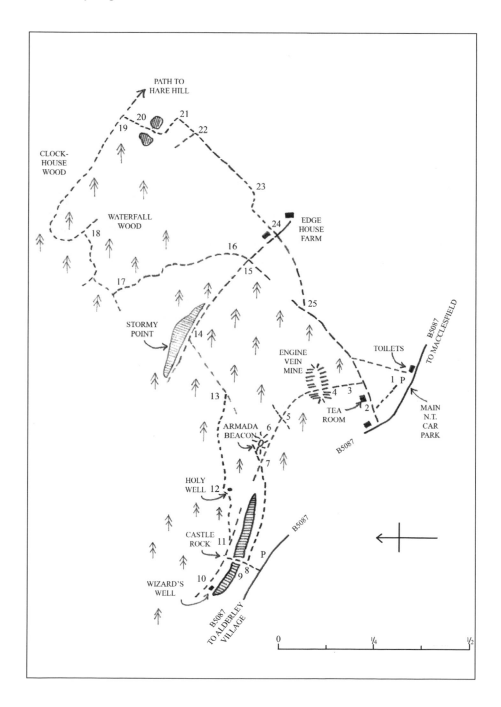

Winter walking at Alderley Edge

in the earth are mines; they have been man-made. People who
explore caves and mines are called pot-holers. You may see some
around the Edge, probably wearing safety helmets with lights on
the front, so they can see where they are going in the darkness
underground. If they have just come out of one of the mines they
will probably be covered with sandy-coloured mud! There are
entrances into the mines on either side of the path, now blocked by
manhole covers.

*The larger mines are all sealed and closed to the public, as they
have been the cause of countless accidents and several deaths
over the years. Supervised trips can be arranged, usually for
Sunday afternoons. The pot-holers have a lock-up just around the
corner from the National Trust Information Room. Ask there for
details.*

5. **Continue ahead into the woods. At the crossroads of paths
   head straight across. Pushchairs bear right, passing the stone**

circle on the right, to emerge at Stormy Point. Continue from
Direction 14.

☺ There are many tall beech trees in this area, and many squirrels
who love to eat the beechnuts that appear on the trees in the
autumn. There are two types of squirrel: grey and red. Red squirrels
are very rare in England now, but grey squirrels are very common.
They are very clever when it comes to food, and often raid bird
tables, hanging bags of bird nuts and even litter bins.

6. At the junction take the shallow steps virtually opposite,
   leading up to the hillock, the site of the Armada Beacon, with a
   stone memorial at the top.

☺ On this small hill there was once a little stone building in which fires
were lit to warn when the country was being invaded. The building
was many hundreds of years old, and it blew down one night during
strong winds. A fire was lit here in 1588 to warn that the Spaniards
were planning to invade. The light of the fire could be seen for miles,
and on hilltops across the land people would light a fire, so that soon
the warning spread all over the country. As it happens the
Spaniards were defeated in a great battle at sea, and never did
manage to invade.

Q: What is the date on the plaque on the site of the beacon?
A: The plaque was presented in 1961.

7. Continue past the beacon, down through the trees towards
   the stone wall on the left. Keep left with the stone wall, then
   follow the upper path with a wire fence/grassy field on your
   left. Continue to the open stone plateau. Take care of the drop!

☺ This is Castle Rock, where supposedly a castle was going to be built,
but in the end it was built at Beeston in West Cheshire instead.
There are views from here over fields and farmland towards
Stockport and Manchester. Over to the left is Manchester Airport,
so you may see several planes taking off or landing.

8. Continue along the path away from Castle Rock. At the junction
   bear right towards the woods.

Escape route: the left turn will lead you to the main road, in an emergency bear left all the way back to the main car park, passing the Wizard restaurant.

9. **Go down the stone steps and bear left along the path. The path winds through the woods, after a short way look out for the stone trough at the base of the overhanging rock on the left.**

Keep close control of small children as there is a slight drop into the woods to the right of the path.

☺ (AT THE WELL) This is the Wizard's Well. Can you see the carving in the rock above the stone basin? It is the face of an old man, and the words:

**"Drink of this and take thy fill
For the water falls by the Wizard's will"**

There is a legend about the Alderley wizard that has been told for hundreds of years, and it goes something like this...

The Legend of The Wizard

Long, long ago, a farmer was walking through the woods in the early morning with a fine white horse, hoping to sell the animal at the market at Macclesfield. From amongst the trees there appeared an old man with a long white beard, dressed in a dark, flowing cloak. The old man offered to buy the horse, but the farmer was greedy, and thought he would make more money at the market, so he refused and continued on his way. The old man called after him, telling him that all day he would get no offers for the horse, but the farmer just laughed and walked on.

In the evening the farmer returned home over the Edge. He had been unable to sell the horse. As if by magic, the old man appeared from the shadows and told the farmer to follow him. He led him to an overhanging rock, where a pair of iron gates appeared from nowhere. The gates swung open and the old man led the way into a cave, going deep down into the earth. In a large cavern there were eleven white horses, all asleep, and there were twelve knights dressed in armour. One of the knights had no horse, so the wizard led the farmer's horse to the twelfth knight and touched its head.

The horse at once fell into a deep sleep. These twelve knights and their twelve horses still sleep on, deep within the hillside, waiting for a day when they will be awakened to fight a great battle and save the country.

And what of the farmer? He was rewarded with as much gold and treasure as he could carry. Since that day the iron gates have never been seen again, though many have tried to find them. A few times over the years, people have claimed to have seen the wizard, so you never know...

10. Return the same way along the path, but avoid going back up the steps, instead keep ahead, passing the base of Castle Rock.

☺ This path passes the sandstone Edge itself. You can see it is red in colour, but in many parts it is covered by grass, moss and lichen. There are beech trees overhanging the path and in some places you can see their roots above the soil, which have to spread a long way to support them in the thin layer of soil over the rock. At some points, you can see the different layers of stone on top of each other.

11.
Take the steps leading downhill on the left. Follow the path as it winds through the trees, stepped in places. Cross the small wooden footbridge then continue up to the Holy Well.

☺ (AT THE HOLY WELL) This is another of Alderley Edge's mysterious wells. It is supposed to have been put here by a farmer, who once owned part of the Edge, and who was jealous because his neighbour owned the part with the Wizard's Well on it. The basin is carved out of sandstone, and the water trickles from deep inside the earth.

12. Immediately to the left of the well there is a path which leads uphill over sandstone rock and exposed tree roots. (Not the level path a short way further top the left.) Continue along this path, to a further stone trough

☺ (AT THE SECOND WELL) Yet another well, collecting water dripping from the rock above. To the right of the trough is a bilberry bush, which has purple berries on it in the summer and autumn. The Edge would have been covered with bushes like this at one time.

13. **Continue along the path and up the steps. At the T-junction bear left along the wide path, over exposed rock and tree roots to the open sandstone plateau.**

☺ This is Stormy Point. No trees grow here, partly because of all the human feet that tread here, and partly because the ground is too rich in minerals. If you look amongst the sand and stones on the floor you might find pieces of green stone, which contain traces of copper. It is this that the miners were looking for. The copper could be melted from the stone, this is called "smelting", and tools or weapons could be made from the metal.

   To the right are the hills of Derbyshire and if you look carefully you might be able to see the tower of Lyme Cage at Lyme Park.

   Also at Stormy Point is a crack in the stone, which is large enough to walk inside. This was once part of a mine, and is now known as the Devil's Grave.

   It is barred off inside, so it is quite safe to enter.

14. **Continue along the top of Stormy Point and follow the main path which is wide and flat, with the Edge on your left.**

☺ There are many tall beech trees on the left, which are fully grown and are probably over 200 years old. Look out for squirrels in the high branches, looking for beechnuts to eat. Squirrels collect lots of nuts and bury some for later in the year, except sometimes they forget where they hid their supply, so the beechnuts are left in the soil and in the spring some of them will begin to grow into new trees.

15. **At the end bear left just before the gate, along a path through the trees which joins a stony trackway leading quite steeply downhill.**

   Escape route/pushchair route: go through the gate and bear right along the trackway, which will take you back to the main car park and Wizard Tea Room.

16. **Follow the trackway as it winds downhill, keep to the main stony trackway, signed for Hare Hill. Follow the path to the**

bottom – here bear right, with the wire fence on your left.

☺ From here there are views back towards the Edge, and you can see the bare sandstone of Stormy Point. There are many different types of trees, and in the autumn the Edge is covered with all shades of brown, yellow and red.

Holy Well

17. The path winds round to a small stream. Step over the stream and bear right, following the stream for a few yards, then the path bears away uphill to the left, over exposed tree roots.

☺ This is Waterfall Wood. On the right is a steep gully with a stream running along the bottom. In very dry weather the stream dries up altogether. This is a quieter part of Alderley Edge, where fewer people come. Keep an eye open for rabbits and squirrels. There are fallen trees in the woods, and some will have fungus growing from their trunks or branches. Fungus can grow on dead or living wood. It often causes the death of a tree.

18. Follow the clear path uphill, stepped in places. At the top bear left. Soon the path winds downhill – it is very clear to follow from now on.

☺ There are many roots across the surface of the soil here. Roots take water to the tree and also food from the soil. They usually spread over a very large area, which helps to keep the tree upright.

19. Keep to the main path, passing a farm on your left. Continue

ahead as the path begins to lead gradually uphill to a junction of
paths.

Q: In the fields on the left there may be horses. What is a young
horse called?
A: A foal

20. **At the junction bear right over the stile and follow the path
along the edge of a farmed field.**

☺ Q: There are often cows in these fields. do you know what a young
cow is called?
A: A calf

21. **Climb the stile and continue ahead between two small ponds,
then bear to the left, with the hedge on your right.**

☺ Q: Look out for sheep in the surrounding fields. You probably know
that a baby sheep is called a lamb, but what are the male and
female sheep called?
A: A female is a ewe, and a male is a ram

22. **Go over the stile in the hedge and follow the narrow path
between fences.**

23. **Climb the stile at the end of the fenced path and continue
ahead along the Sandy Farm trackway, heading gradually uphill
towards farm buildings.**

☺ On the left are open fields and views to the hills, including
Shuttlingsloe, which looks like an upturned basin, and is one of the
highest points in Cheshire. It can be seen from all over the county.

24. **At the top of the trackway climb the stile and bear right to a
further stile, after which keep left, uphill, passing the farm
buildings on the far left.**

Q: On the right is a brick cottage with a roof of stone. How many
chimneys does it have?
A: Two

25. Go through the gate and continue ahead. Cross the farm driveway and continue along the narrow fenced footpath between fields heading towards the trees of Alderley Edge.

26. After the fenced path bear left along the trackway. After a short way there is a stile on the left leading back to the car park, or continue ahead to the Wizard Tea Room.

Alderley Edge Checklist

☐ A MINE SHAFT	☐ A DOG
☐ A WATERFALL	☐ A FALLEN TREE
☐ A HORSE	☐ A COW
☐ A FARMHOUSE	☐ A FOOTBRIDGE
☐ SOMEONE WITH A WALKING STICK	☐ A TREE WITH BERRIES
☐ A BLACKBERRY BUSH	☐ A THATCHED ROOF

2. Aldford

This is a short walk (with options to make it longer) around the village of Aldford and the surrounding countryside, owned mainly by the Duke of Westminster, whose home is nearby Eaton Hall. A varied and very pleasant walk for a Sunday afternoon at any time of the year.

Starting point	Aldford Church (SJ419595) the village is well signed from the B5130 Chester to Farndon road. If approaching from the Chester direction bear right into the village, and there is a car park a short way along on the left, before you reach the church
By bus	Services between Chester and Farndon. Bus stops on the B-road just outside the village
Distance	A gentle 1½ (with no escape routes). The walk can be extended by continuing further along both sides of the river, but returning the same way to continue with the circular route
Terrain	Mainly flat footpaths, trackways and village streets
Maps	OS Landranger 117
Public toilets	None
Refreshments	Pub on the main road, a short walk from the village
Pushchairs	Around the village only

☺ (IN THE VILLAGE) This is the village of Aldford, which means "old ford". A "ford" is a type of crossing place over a river, a place where the water is shallow and can be driven or waded across. At one time

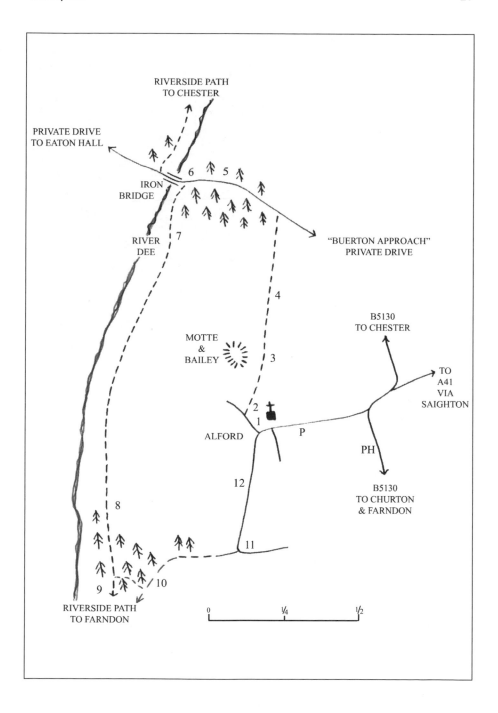

RIVERSIDE PATH
TO CHESTER

PRIVATE DRIVE
TO EATON HALL

6 5

IRON
BRIDGE

"BUERTON APPROACH"
PRIVATE DRIVE

RIVER
DEE 7

4

B5130
TO CHESTER

MOTTE
&
BAILEY 3

TO
A41
VIA
SAIGHTON

2

1

ALFORD P

PH

12

B5130
TO CHURTON
& FARNDON

8

11

9 10

RIVERSIDE PATH
TO FARNDON

0   ¼   ½

there must have been a crossing from here over the River Dee, which runs nearby.

If you look around, you can see that most of the houses are similar, built of brick with diamond patterns below the bedroom windows. Some of the houses have square chimneys and some have round ones.

This village and several others in the area (Saighton, Eccleston and Pulford) are estate villages of Eaton Hall, which is on the other side of the river. This means they belonged to the hall, and the villagers would have to pay rent for their

Aldford Boathouse

homes. Eaton Hall is the home of the Duke of Westminster. A Duke is a title which is passed down through the family, so that when one Duke dies, the eldest son will then become the next Duke, so there have been lots of Dukes of Westminster living at the Hall. It was the first Duke who had this village built nearly 150 years ago. More houses were added a hundred years ago. Can you see any plaques with dates on?

1. **Enter the churchyard via the main gates, opposite the village stores.**

☺ This is the church of Saint John the Baptist. It has a sandstone tower with a spire on top. There is also a strange smaller tower attached to the side of the main tower with tiny windows in it. This has stairs in it, which lead up to the bells. If you look up at the main tower you will see what looks like an arched window, but instead of glass in it, there are strips of wood. The bells are inside here, and the gaps between the wooden strips let the sound out. They also let birds and bats in. Bats are like winged mice, and many people are frightened of them, though they are quite harmless. They are "nocturnal" animals, which means they only come out at night, when it's dark. During the day they sleep hanging upside down in the roofs of barns, old buildings and church towers.

Q: Can you find the tallest monument at the front of the church? It should be quite easy to spot. It is in memory of one of the Dukes of Westminster. In which year was it restored?
A: 1901, as it says at the end of the plaque

Just to the left of the church door there is an old sundial. This was used for telling the time. The sun casts a shadow on the "clockface", and the shadow moves throughout the day. You will have noticed that the sun seems to move in the sky. It rises in the east in the morning, and sets in the west at night. That is why it might be sunny in your bedroom in the morning, but not in the afternoon, or the other way round.

Aldford Church

2. **Bear to the left of the tower to a set of steps leading over the
   wall. Take the white wooden gate on the immediate right and
   follow the path ahead across the field, through the edge of the
   earthwork. Keep to the path as it bears around to the left, with
   the fence on your left.**

☺ Over on the left is a huge bank and ditch, which was once part of a
"motte and bailey", which was a sort of castle. It was built here long
before the village. The bank and ditch were for protection.
Neighbouring villagers weren't always very friendly, and might
decide to steal your land or belongings. Also, the Welsh border is
close by, and groups of Welsh robbers would sometimes come over
and take whatever they could get their hands on. On the "island" in
the middle of the ditch there would have been wooden buildings, and
the ditch would have been full of water. It is very old, and was built
at least 800 years ago.
   Near the castle there is a large oak tree, which must also be
quite old, because its trunk is very wide. It is hollow inside, but the
tree is still alive. If you are small enough you could crawl inside and
stand up.

3. **Continue to the gate, go through and keep straight ahead across
   the open field.**

☺ In the distance ahead, you should be able to see a very tall tower
rising over the treetops, which looks a bit like the top of a rocket.
It is in fact the clock tower of the chapel at Eaton Hall, the home of
the Duke of Westminster, the owner of the village. It is 175 feet
high, which is very high, even for a church steeple.

4. **The path leads slightly downhill to a gate (next to a five bar
   gate) in the bottom right corner of the field. Go through and
   bear left along the driveway.**

☺ On both sides now there are woods, made up of many different trees,
such as sycamore and oak. Acorns are the fruit of the oak tree. You
have probably seen them many times before. At one time they were
collected and fed to pigs.Today they can be roasted and ground to
make a coffee-like drink. The wood from the oak tree is very strong
and was often used for building the frames of houses.

There are also rhododendron bushes in the woods, which have colourful flowers in the spring and summer, and they do not lose their dark green, oval leaves in the winter, so they are called "evergreens", because they are green all the year round. Another familiar evergreen is holly. There are several holly bushes in the woods, and some of them have red berries in the autumn. A short way ahead look out for yet another evergreen, a tall tree called a "yew". It has a soft, flaky bark and dark green leaves, which are small and thin, like needles. Like holly, many yews have red berries, which are poisonous. See if you can spot a yew tree.

5. Continue to the bridge.

☺ This bridge is made of iron, a type of metal, and it crosses the River Dee, which flows through the city of Chester, and then out to the sea. The bridge was built in 1824 for Eaton Hall, nearby, to carry one of its many long driveways. The two men responsible for building the bridge were called William Hazledean and William Stuttle. Can you find their names on the bridge?

On the opposite bank is a black and white building you could see across the fields. Only the top half of the house is black and white. The bottom half is built of brick. It is part of the Eaton Hall estate and has the same diamond patterns in the brickwork as many of the houses in the village.

To extend the route it is permissible to cross the bridge, and a footpath leads off to the right through the trees and follows the river to the estate village of Eccleston, then on for some way towards Chester. Return the same way to the bridge and continue with the route.

6. Bear left directly before the bridge, along a signed footpath which runs close to the river.

☺ There are more yew trees along the path at this point, some of which have berries.

7. Go through the metal kissing gate and continue straight ahead. The path runs along the river bank but frequently zig-zags to the edge of the field where the river bank is impassable. Keep

as close to the river as possible at all times.

☺ You should be able to see the tall spire of the church across the fields from here. Occasionally you should be able to see the river, but sometimes it will be hidden by all the tall plants that grow on the bank, like nettles which can sting you, as you probably know, and prickly thistles which have purple flowering heads in the summer. Next time you have any pound coins, look at them, as some show a thistle on one side. The thistle is the "emblem" of Scotland. An emblem is a picture which is used as a sort of badge. The leek is the emblem of Wales and the red rose is the emblem of England.

Aldford Bridge over the River Dee

Q: Look out for a sign almost hidden by the tall plants. What is the speed limit for boats on the water?
A: 6 mph; 6 miles per hour

A little way ahead there is a farm over on the left, and you can probably see the church steeple again over the top of it. There is a hay barn, which in the autumn and winter should be full of hay. Hay is a tall grass which is grown for winter food for cows and horses.
        There are several willow trees close to the river and there are any more on the other side, which lean right over the water. Can you recognise them? Willows have long, narrow, oval-shaped leaves and the lower branches used to be collected to make baskets.

8. **Continue along the river bank for some way (about half a mile) to the end of the field, where there is an area of fenced wood-**

land with a stile. Cross over and continue through the woods. Keep right, crossing a bridge over a stream. Continue ahead. Look out for a pathway to the left (currently unsigned) which will lead you away from the river and in a short way to a bridge over a drainage ditch to a farmer's trackway.

9. Bear left along the track, which soon bears around to the right and leads slightly uphill towards the village.

☺ There are high hedges on both sides of the trackway, made up of many wild plants like prickly hawthorns, and a type of climbing plant which has started to cover the other bushes. Along the grassy banks you may see rabbit burrows, or larger holes made by badgers, with piles of soft sand outside the entrance, which the badgers have scraped out with their strong claws. Badgers, like bats, are nocturnal, they only come out at night, so it is unlikely you will see one.

10. Keep straight ahead, avoiding all other trackways. Go through the five bar gate across the track and continue ahead.

☺ Q: There is a weathervane on top of a building on the right. A weathervane points in the direction the wind is blowing. What type of animal is on top of this one?
   A: A bird, probably a grouse

11. Bear left along the quiet village street.

☺ Q: The first houses on the left are a pair of semi-detached cottages. "Semi-detached" means there are two houses joined together. They are the most common type of houses in towns and cities. These cottages are built of plain bricks, and there are dates over the doors, which tell you when they were built. What is the date?
   A: 1859

This is School Lane, and not surprisingly, there was once a school here. Perhaps you can tell which was the school building?

   Q: Look out on the left for the old "thatched" cottage; that is a house with a roof made of straw, which is how most roofs would be made at one time. There is a model bird sitting in the middle of the roof. How many tall chimneys are there on the cottage?

A: Four

You will pass other semi-detached cottages, with dates of 1856 and 1858. As you might have noticed by now, most of the village was built around that time, in the 1850's, though there are a few houses which are older.

Ahead is the church tower, which should tell you that this is the end of the walk.

12. **Bear right to the church gates/starting point and car park.**

Aldford Checklist

☐	A "WEATHERVANE"	☐	A BLACK AND WHITE COW
☐	A TELEPHONE BOX	☐	A TRACTOR
☐	AN IRON BRIDGE	☐	A WHITE GATE
☐	A BLACK AND WHITE COTTAGE	☐	A POST BOX
☐	A STINGING NETTLE	☐	A RABBIT HOLE
☐	A HOLLY BUSH	☐	A DOG

3. Audlem

Audlem is a pleasant small town in South Cheshire, and close by is the Shropshire Union Canal, well known for its many locks, of which there are fifteen in the immediate area. The surrounding countryside is relatively flat; an attractive patchwork of hedged fields and pastures. This route takes in the town, the countryside and the canal. A very rewarding half day walk, or longer if you include a picnic stop. (There are picnic tables at certain points along the canal and a playground at the end.)

Starting point	Car park in the centre of the village, (SJ659437) well signed, just off Cheshire Street/A529. From the main village street, turn off by the church and the car park is a short way on the left
By bus	Services from Crewe and Nantwich to village centre
Distance	Entire route: just under 6 miles Shorter route: 3 miles
Terrain	Almost entirely flat paths through pleasant farmed fields and along the canal towpath. a short distance along lanes
Maps	OS Explorer 257 or Landranger 118
Public toilets	In the car park/starting point (there is a nominal entrance charge) including disabled facilities
Refreshments	Pubs, cafes etc in village
Pushchairs	Not suitable, except along canal towpath

1. **From the car park bear right along Cheshire Street towards the centre of the village.**

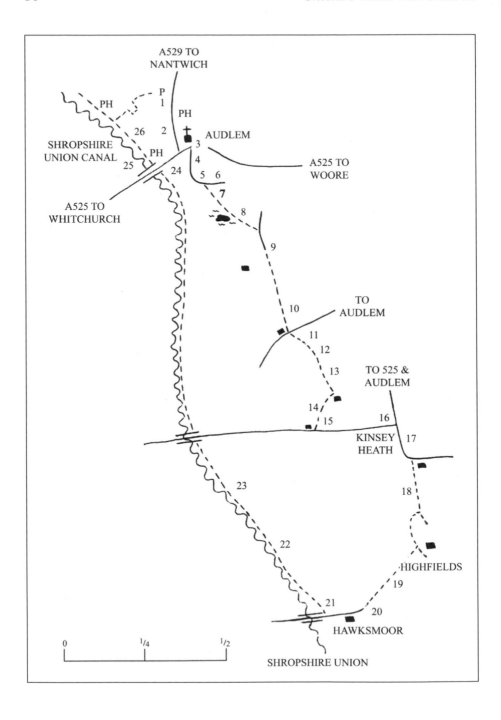

☺ Q: What animal is the pub named after?
A: A lamb

2. Carefully cross the road and climb the steps to the church.

☺ This is Saint James' Church and the oldest parts are between seven and eight hundred years old. It is built of local sandstone, and if you look carefully you can see where some of the large, square sandstone blocks have been replaced as they have become worn and damaged. The church is built on a slight hill and from the surrounding countryside the tower can be seen rising above the roofs of the little town.

Q: See if you can find out in which year the clock was "installed" in the tower.
A: There is a plaque on the tower which will give you the answer. The clock was installed for the "coronation" or crowning of King George V and Queen Mary on 22 June 1911.

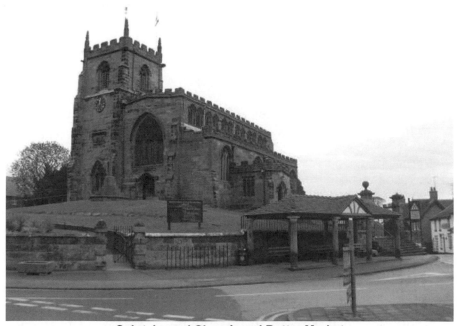

Saint James' Church and Butter Market

3. **Go down the steps to the main gates of the church.**

☺ At the bottom of the steps is a building which looks a bit like a bus shelter, and in fact, that is just what it's now used for. At one time it was the town's butter market, and was built in 1733.

4. **Cross the main village street and go down the narrow road (Vicarage Lane) directly opposite the church gates.**

5. **Follow the lane downhill. It soon curves to the left, after which take the footpath off to the right, over the grass. Cross over the stream.**

☺ On the right just before the bridge there is a row of lime trees, which have large, heart-shaped leaves. Audlem gets its name from this type of tree. The town was originally known as Alda's Lime. Alda was a person, and over the years the name has been shortened and changed slightly, to become Audlem.

6. **Go over the bridge and keep straight ahead, climbing to the top of the grassy hill.**

☺ From the top of the hill, if you turn round you will have fine views of the town. Notice how the church tower can be seen clearly over the rooftops of the shops and houses.

7. **Continue across the grassy field, heading for a stile in the far right corner.**

☺ You might see a swamp over on the right, with many reeds and bulrushes around its edges. Bulrushes have brown cigar-shaped "pods" which are full of tiny seeds. In the springtime the pods burst and the seeds are blown away by the wind, so that they might find some soil and begin to grow. Bulrushes like clean, shallow water, like this.

8. **Cross the stile and continue left to the tarmac driveway. Bear right along the driveway towards the farm buildings. Follow the driveway between the farmhouse and pre-fab outbuildings. Continue ahead between grassy fields.**

☺ There is an old corrugated iron hay barn on the right, which the farmer will store hay in, to stop it getting wet and going rotten in the bad winter weather. Hay is tall grass which can be used for winter food for cows and horses. In the late summer you might see hay being cut and made into big rolls. It is then left out in the sun for several days to dry out before it is brought into the barns.

9. **After the old haybarn the drive bears to the right to another farmhouse – instead keep straight ahead along a rough track-way between farmed fields.**

☺ In the autumn the trees and bushes have many berries, which carry their seeds. Towards the end of the trackway there is a hedgerow with several plants that have brightly coloured fruit or berries. If it is late summer or autumn, see if you can spot any. Damsons are purple plums, a bit bigger than a marble. Hawthorns have sharp thorns and small, blood-red berries. Rosehips are orangey-red and look a bit like small tomatoes.

10. **At the end of the track climb the stile beside the five bar gate and take the footpath directly over the lane.**

   Escape route: bear right along the lane and right at the junction. Continue to the canal. Take the gate on the left before the bridge and bear right along the towpath. Continue with the route from Direction 24.

☺ Q: What is the name of the cottage on the lane to the right of the stile?
   A: Holly Cottage

11. **Follow the path straight ahead with the hedge on your right.**

☺ Again there are many berries in the hedgerows. These can be eaten by birds and small animals through the cold winter, when there is little else to eat, but don't you try eating any! Even if the ground is covered with snow, the berries are all brightly coloured and can easily be found by hungry animals and birds.
   Some birds "migrate" in the winter. This means they fly away to other countries where it is warmer, like Africa. Some birds stay

here and brave the cold weather though. Sparrows and robins can be seen all the year round. They need a lot to eat in the winter to keep them alive, so why not put some food out for them at home, especially nuts, which have a lot of fat in them which helps to keep them warm.

12. **Towards the end of the field bear left, cutting across the middle of the field towards a stile in the far left corner.**

13. **Cross the stile and continue straight ahead, keeping to the edge of the field. At the end of the field the path bears to the right in front of a house. A short way after the house take the stile on the left. Bear diagonally right.**

☺ Here there is another small pond. In the summer it is surrounded by yellow flowers which attract butterflies and other insects, like dragonflies, which are often bright blue and have long wings and thin bodies. They can often be seen hovering close to the surface of the water.

Q: Butterflies lay their eggs on leaves. When they hatch, it isn't a butterfly that crawls out. Do you know what it is?

A: A caterpillar. Caterpillars eat as many green leaves as they can, then they make themselves a "cocoon" or "chrysalis", which is a sort of small furry egg. Inside the cocoon they begin to change, and when they finally break their way out they have grown wings and have become a butterfly.

14. **Pass the pond on the right and continue ahead to a metal kissing gate in the hedge. Cross the field to a stile in the right corner.**

☺ Look out for old baths in the fields, which are used for cows to drink from. A thirsty cow can drink huge amounts of water; up to a bathful every day!

Q: Next to the stile (ON THE RIGHT) is Kinsey House. What is the date on the front of the building?

A: 1902

Escape route: to cut the route in half bear right along the lane.
Avoid the turning to the right and continue ahead to the canal.
Go through the gate on the left before the bridge. Bear right along
the towpath, continuing with Direction 24.

15. Bear left along the lane.

☺ Q: You should soon pass a row of brick cottages. One of them is
named after a flower, and one is named after a tree. What
are their two names?

A: Rose Cottage and Oak Cottage

16. Avoid the footpath to the right and continue to the T-junction. Bear right along Woodhouse Lane.

☺ Q: Further on there is a black and white metal road sign next to
a post box. How far are Audlem and Nantwich from here?

Frozen Canal

A: As it says on the sign, Audlem is 1 mile and Nantwich is 8 miles away.

Q: After a short way there is a gate on the left, and a driveway with tall pine trees along it. The drive leads to a house. What is its name?

A: The unusual name can be found on the gate. "Kynsal Lodge"

17. **Soon the lane begins to bear to the left. On the corner there is a black and white house. Take the unsigned driveway directly before the house, crossing the cattle grid and continuing ahead.**

☺ Over on the left is a mixed woodland, made up of many different types of trees, which are very colourful in the autumn. In the fields there will probably be many cows, grazing. They pull the grass up with their strong, rough tongues and seem to chew almost all the time.

18. **When the driveway splits, bear right. At the crossroads of farm driveways continue straight across, over another cattle grid. After a short way the drive bears around to the left, towards an attractive black and white manor house – here, go through the metal gate on the right between wire fences. Keep straight ahead towards a metal gate in the far right corner of the field.**

☺ Over on the left is a large house with a wooden frame and white panels, and a lot of tall brick chimneys. It is called Highfields and it was built in 1615, so it is very old.

19. **Go through the metal gate and keep straight ahead along a clear rutted trackway.**

☺ Here there are large, open fields which may have crops in them, such as wheat, corn, potatoes or possibly green vegetables like cabbage. If it is autumn you may see a tractor ploughing the field. In the spring you may see a tractor spreading seeds. In the late summer you may see a farmer "harvesting" or collecting the crop, using tractors and other machines. At one time the crops had to be collected by hand, and as you can imagine, it was a very long job.

20. **Keep straight ahead. The track becomes a concrete driveway**

and leads towards farm buildings. Keep straight ahead between the barns and farmhouse, and continue along the lane. (There are many five bar gates which may be closed, but go through or over, keeping ahead at all times.)

☺ Q: Look out for the farmhouse on the left after the barns. How many chimneys are there on the main roof?
A: Three

21. A short way along the lane you will come to a canal bridge. Go through the gate on the right before the bridge, down the steps and bear right along the towpath (so the canal is on your left).

☺ Q: If you look back at the bridge you will see it has a number on it. What number is it?
A: All the bridges along the canal are numbered, so people using the canal know where they are. This bridge is number 72.

Audlem Lock and Bridge

The water is almost chocolate coloured. When the canals were built they were dug out by men with spades, as there were no diggers or machines in those days. The bottom and sides of the canal were then lined with a thick clay, which is watertight, so the water could not sink into the soil. It is the clay that has coloured the water.

There are many wild plants growing along the path, like nettles, which you will probably know quite well, because they can sting you. There are also thistles, which are quite tall and prickly, and have purple flowers. And there is hogweed, which is also tall, and has clusters of white flowers in the spring and summer.

Look out for the number as you approach the next bridge, which should be number 73.

22. Pass under the bridge and continue along the towpath.

☺ After the bridge there is a sandy bank alongside the path, with many blackberry bushes and hawthorns growing on it. Can you see any holes in the bank? The smaller ones will be rabbit burrows, but there are also larger holes with piles of sand outside them. These are likely to have been made by badgers. You have probably never seen a living badger, as they are "nocturnal" animals, which means they only usually come out at night. They have black and white heads and greyish bodies. A badger hole is called a "sett", which is usually made up of many long tunnels, all joined together, with several different entrances. Badgers, unlike many wild animals, live in family groups, even when they are grown up.

A little further on, there are views across the water to the fields on the other side, where you might see horses grazing.

Q: Look out for an old black and white signpost alongside the path. The one you saw earlier was for people using the road. This one is for people using the canal. How far is to Nantwich from here?

A: 8 miles, which is the same as on the road sign.

23. Pass under all subsequent bridges and continue ahead.

☺ Once you have gone under bridge 74 there are trees on both sides of the canal, shading the water. They are mainly sycamores, which you may recognise. They are quite common in parks and gardens.

A little further along you might notice there are metal rings in the ground where boats can be tied up. Perhaps there are some boats here now. Canal boats are long and narrow, so it isn't surprising that they are called "narrow boats". Some people live on narrow boats, but usually they are just used for relaxing boating holidays.

Further along you will come to the first of the canal "locks". A "lock" is a kind of "lift" for boats. The canal is moving downhill towards the flat Cheshire Plain, and the locks are like a series of steps, which lower the narrow boats gently up or downhill. If you are lucky, you might see one of them in use. (The best time is a summer afternoon at the week-end). There are no less than 15 locks along this part of the canal, so you will pass many more of them before the end of the walk. Look out for bridge 75.

Soon there are several more locks. Notice as you pass, that the water after each lock is lower than the water before it, as the canal heads downhill towards the Plain. There may be boats using the locks, which can fit two in at a time. There may also be boats tied up along the edge of the canal. They are often very colourful and some have names painted on them.

After bridge 76 and 77 the locks are fairly close together.

24. **When nearly in Audlem there are houses on the right. Go under the road bridge (78).**

☺ The pub high up on the right is called the Bridge Inn. It has been a pub for many years, and was always popular with the boatmen. It still is, for that matter.

25. **Go up the steps on the right to Audlem Mill Canal Shop, then continue towards the Shroppie Fly Inn.**

☺ **(AT THE CANAL AND NEEDLEWORK SHOP)** This building is now a shop selling everything for canal boats and boating holidays, including gifts and souvenirs. At one time it was a mill, grinding grain, like wheat, into flour, which could then be made into bread. The canal would have been used to bring the grain to the mill, and then take sacks of flour to other towns to sell to bakeries.

Further ahead is a pub called the "Shroppie Fly". The name has nothing to do with flies at all. "Fly Boats" were fast boats for carrying people, and "Shroppie" is a sort of local nickname for the canal, which is properly called the "Shropshire Union Canal". The pub was once a warehouse, storing goods brought by the canal. Notice it still has a crane outside, which was used for hauling heavy sacks of coal or potatoes on and off the boats.

26. Head into the car park of the Shroppie Fly and bear right. From the back right corner there are a set of steps leading uphill into the trees. Follow the path to the sports field and cross to the car park and starting point.

    There is a playground to the right of the sports field, directly before the car park.

Audlem Checklist

☐ A CHURCH TOWER	☐ A POST BOX
☐ A COW	☐ A TRACTOR
☐ A RABBIT OR HARE	☐ A BIRD'S FEATHER
☐ A POND	☐ A CANAL BOAT
☐ A CRANE OR WINCH	☐ A HORSE
☐ BERRIES ON A TREE (OR BLOSSOM IN SPRING)	☐ A BRICK BRIDGE

4. Barthomley

Barthomley is a quiet village in the south-east of the County. It was once the scene of much fighting during the civil war, when the villagers barricaded themselves in the church tower. They were smoked out by the King's men and a dozen were executed. This violent event and the church itself appear in Alan Garner's complex but brilliant novel, "Red Shift".

The surrounding countryside is rural and largely unspoilt, despite the proximity of the motorway.

Starting point	**The church of Saint Bertoline, Barthomley. (SJ767524). Car parking space along the lane near to the White Lion Inn, or at the front entrance to the church. Barthomley is close to junction 16 of the M6 and is well signed. Take the B5078 and then the first left turning to take you straight into the village**
By bus	**From Crewe. Stops in the village**
Distance	**Entire route: 3 miles**
Terrain	**Mainly flat footpaths across farmed fields**
Maps	**OS explorer 257 or Landranger 118**
Public toilets	**No public toilets. Facilities in pub for patrons only**
Refreshments	**The White Lion Inn, Barthomley**
Pushchairs	**Unsuitable**

☺ (FROM THE DRIVEWAY IN FRONT OF THE CHURCH) This is the Church of Saint Bertoline. It was built several hundred years ago, but was restored in the last century. Like many churches, it is built on a slight hill overlooking the village, so that its tower could be

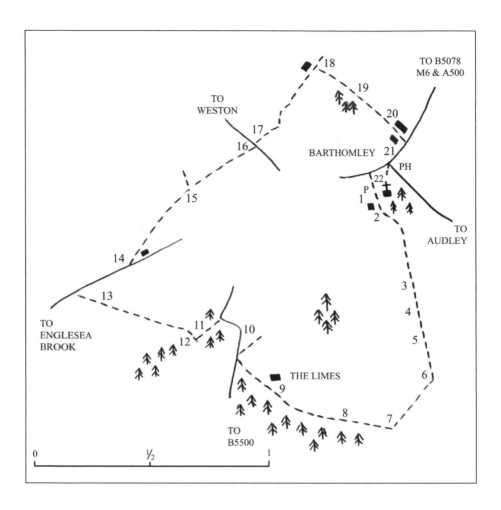

seen from miles away. The village has its fair share of ghost stories. There is supposed to be the spirit of a dog which runs close to the church after sunset as the shadows are falling and the moon is rising in the sky. When it is seen it is supposed to mean bad luck is on the way.

1. **From the steps leading up to the church, continue up the driveway, passing the modern rectory on the right and the Church Hall on the left. Continue ahead via a narrow path alongside the hedge, passing a small pond on your left.**

☺ Hidden away in the trees there is a small, muddy pond with many reeds growing on the far side. This quiet spot gives shelter and drinking water for many birds, which you may hear scuttling away between the undergrowth as you approach. Some of the trees have

ivy growing on them. Ivy is a climbing plant, which has tiny "suckers" on it to help it cling to walls or the bark of trees. It can cover whole areas of woodland. The leaves stay green all year and are often used in Christmas decorations.

2. **The path rounds the pond to a stile on the right. Cross the stile and bear left to a further stile, taking you into open fields.**

☺ The woods on the left are made up of many different types of tree, including willows which like damp ground. There are also

Saint Bertoline Church

some elderberry trees, which have clusters of small black berries in the late summer and autumn. See how many trees you can recognise.

3. **Continue straight across the field, slightly uphill, to a further stile in a hedge, towards the right corner of the field.**

☺ There is another small pond in the middle of the field. Are there any ducks on it?

4. **Once over the stile continue straight ahead, again there is a slight climb towards the end of the field. Cross the next stile and again continue straight across the field.**

☺ You may see many rabbit holes on your walk today. Rabbits live in family groups. Their holes are called "burrows", or a lot of holes together are called a "warren". Rabbits eat grass, leaves and green shoots.

5. **This smaller field drops down slightly to the next stile, after which the path climbs gently, with a hawthorn hedge on the left.**

☺ Over on the right is a farm called "The Limes". Perhaps the field you are walking through has been planted with a crop, such as wheat or corn. Wheat is tall, like yellow grass. Corn is even taller with long green leaves. Can you think of any types of food that are made from wheat or corn?

6. **Climb the steps to the stile and this time bear right along the edge of the field.**

☺ At about this point you will be crossing the border from Cheshire into the neighbouring county of Staffordshire. (It doesn't look any different, does it?) This is quite a large field. At one time most of the fields in England were small and surrounded by colourful hedgerows, but today, many trees and hedgerows have been chopped down so that it is easier for the farmer to use modern machines to plough, plant and collect the crops. Unfortunately, this means that the homes of many animals, birds and insects are destroyed.
   The country was once completely covered with trees, except for the very highest mountains. Over thousands of years, people have cut down the trees for wood, or to make fields for farming or space for building. There are now far fewer areas covered with trees and woodland.

7. **A stile in the lower right corner of the field leads down into the woods. Cross the bridge and follow the steps up to a further stile. Continue ahead with the woods on your left.**

☺ Again, these are mixed woodlands, and there are many elderberry trees with their clusters of dark berries (in autumn) and many oak trees, which shower the ground with acorns and provide winter food for squirrels. On the ground between the trees there are many ferns which grow well in poor, sandy soil.

8. **Keep the woods on your left and cross various stiles in close succession.**

☺ Q: This is Limes Farm again. How many chimney pots can you

count on the farmhouse?
A: Five

9. After you have passed the farm (over on your right) take the
    stile in the wooden fence into a grassy horse paddock.
    Continue straight ahead – roughly parallel to the farm
    driveway over on the right. At the end of the field take the
    stile onto the lane, bear right.

    *Escape route: instead of crossing the stile bear right to a further
    stile onto the driveway of Limes Farm, and take the footpath
    opposite, which will lead you back across the fields to the church.*

10. Continue along the lane for a short distance. There is a narrow
    grass verge for part of the way. Take the footpath off to the
    left.

    *Escape route: Continue along the lane and bear right at the
    junction, which will take you back to Barthomley.*

11. Follow the path through the area of woodland. Keep to the
    main path, which bears around to the left between small ponds.

☺   Again there are many oak trees, as well as blackberries and ferns.
    There are several small bogs on either side of the path. Make sure
    you don't fall in!

12. Cross the bridge and stile and bear right to a further stile and
    bridge. Continue ahead across the farmed field – begin to bear
    to the left, so you pass close by the pond (on your left) and
    continue to the far left corner of the field.

☺   Look out for the swampy area on the left surrounded by trees.
    There are many elderberry trees, and also several crab apple trees.
    These have very small apples, about the size of large cherries. They
    are very bitter and can give you stomach ache, so don't try eating
    one! You should also pass a small round pond with lilies floating on
    the water. There are many plants growing around its edges, like
    nettles, dock (tall with large oval leaves) and rosebay willow herb,
    which has pink flowers.

13. **In the left corner of the field there is a stile. Cross this and bear right along the hedge to the lane. Bear right along the lane.**

☺ Q: On your right, there is a high hedge, made mainly out of a plant that has dark green, prickly leaves. What is it called?

   A: Holly. It is often used as part of Christmas decorations, because it stays green all year round and some types have bright red berries in the winter. You might have heard the Christmas carol, "The Holly and the Ivy". Ivy is another plant which stays green all year round.

14. **Take the trackway off to the left directly before the next house. It passes behind the house and then between fields.**

☺ This is a "bridleway" which means it can be used by horses. You might see horses' hoofprints in the ground. You might also see shoe or boot prints. See which is the largest print you can find.

15. **Avoid the footpath to the left and continue ahead.**

☺ There are often horses grazing in the fields along this path. Over on the right you should be able to see the back of a farm (Old Hall Farm) and if you look carefully you might see the tower of the church over the treetops.

16. **Carefully cross the lane and take the stile opposite.**

Escape route: Bear right along the lane and then left at the junction, which will take you back to the village.

17. **From the stile bear diagonally left and cross over the small stream via the wooden bridge. Continue ahead, aiming for the red brick farm buildings, then follow the edge of the field, with the hedge on your left.**

☺ You might be able to hear the sound of the motorway and main roads again. On the right are the houses of the village of Barthomley, and on the left are a couple of old brick stables, which have special doors, so that the top part could be left open for the horses to see out.

18. You should come to a stile on the left. Do not cross the stile, but at this point bear right, straight across the field, heading for the tower of the church.

19. Pass the outcrop of trees on your right (Parson's Pit – an old fishing pond) and continue to a corner of the field (this is an irregular shaped field and has many corners!) where there is a stile. Cross this and follow the path which leads between attractive cottages.

☺ Q: On your right you should pass a neat square of very short grass. What do you think it is used for?
A: It's the village bowling green, where people play bowls

20. Keep straight ahead, which will bring you down to the village. Bear right along the pavement.

White Lion Inn

☺ In the hedge on the right is a well; water runs from a pipe into a stone trough. You can see the water is very clear.

    Q: Like many of the houses in Barthomley, the village inn is black and white. What is it called?

    A: The White Lion

21. Carefully cross the road and climb the church steps.

☺ In the churchyard there are several yew trees. See if you can spot one. They have small, dark green leaves, flaky reddish-brown bark and sometimes red berries.

22. Cross the graveyard to the main steps to return to the Church car park and starting point.

Barthomley Checklist

☐ A CHURCH TOWER	☐ A POND WITH REEDS
☐ A BLACK AND WHITE COTTAGE	☐ A GRAVESTONE
☐ A BLACK AND WHITE COW	☐ A RABBIT
☐ A BIRD'S FEATHER	☐ A TRACTOR
☐ A HORSE	☐ A STREAM
☐ A FIELD OF WHEAT OR CORN	☐ A DOG

5. Big Mere and Marbury
(near Whitchurch)

Not to be confused with Marbury near Northwich. This Marbury is an attractive village overlooking Big Mere and the gentle hills that rise towards the Shropshire border. Good views, a large resident wildfowl population and a stroll along the canal bank make this a varied and very pleasant walk.

Starting point	Lay-by at Willey Moor on the A49, a couple of miles north of Whitchurch (SJ539466)
By rail	The nearest station is at Whitchurch, 2 miles to the south
Distance	Entire route: 6 miles
Terrain	Canal towpaths and footpaths over some hilly areas
Maps	OS explorer 257 or Landranger 117
Public toilets	No public toilets. facilities at 2 pubs for patrons only
Refreshments	Pubs
Pushchairs	A mile each way along the towpath. The rest of the route is unsuitable

1. From the lay-by head for the bridge that crosses over the canal. On the west-side of the road there is a narrow path leading down to the canal. Bear right along the towpath.

☺ This is part of the Shropshire Union Canal. There are canals all over the country. Perhaps there is one near where you live. They are man-made waterways which were built for moving goods such as coal or potatoes from one place to another.

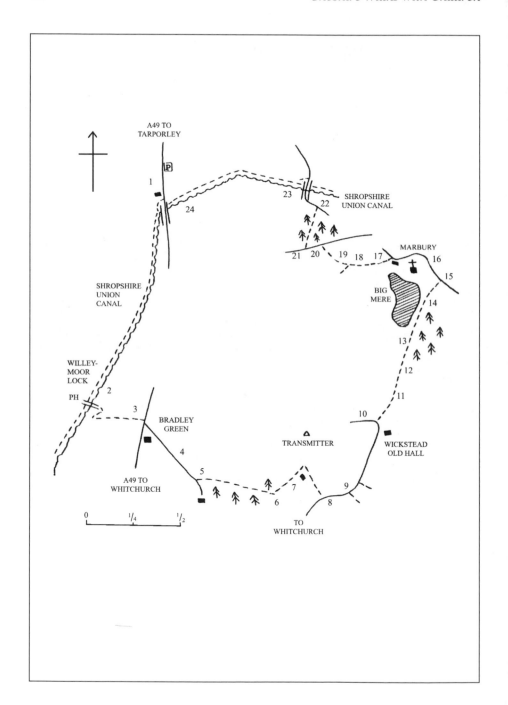

Shropshire Union Canal

Along the path there are metal posts for tying boats to, so that they don't float away. Canal boats are long and are called "narrowboats". Some people live on them, but most are used for holidays.

Very soon you should come across the first "lock". Because the land isn't always flat, sometimes a canal goes from high country to low country, and a lock is used to lower or raise a boat. If you look at the level of the water on each side of the lock, you will see that one side is higher than the other. If you are lucky, you may see a boat using the lock (weekend afternoons are usually the best time) and you will see how it works. There is no electricity involved. It works by the power of the water.

Q: The hedgerow along the path is made up of many different plants. Some of these plants have blossom in the spring and berries in the autumn. Can you recognise any of them?
A: Elderberries are small and black. Rosehips are red, and about the size of cherries. Hawthorn berries are red, but smaller.

Also along the path there are prickly thistles and very tall reeds, which you will have to walk between.

You will soon come to another lock with a pub next to it, which was once a lock-keeper's cottage and stable block, where horses slept. It is a popular stopping place for the people on the narrowboats, so you may see a long line of boats tied up here, where they have probably spent the night.

This is Willeymoor Lock, and the pub is Willeymoor Lock Tavern, which seems logical enough. There are seats outside and a family room inside as well.

2.   **At the pub, cross the bridge over the canal. Turn right, then cross a second bridge over the canal overflow. Follow the path for a short way, then cross back (yet again) over a further small bridge to the stile. Cross the stile and continue straight ahead, towards the road – keeping to the edge of the field.**

The Swan Inn and village green, Marbury

3. **Climb the stile onto the road and carefully cross. Bear right for a short way, then turn left down Bradeley Green Lane.**

☺ Q: There is a "T" sign at the start of this lane. You have probably
           seen signs like this quite often, especially in the town, but do you
           know what it means?
   A: It means the road is a dead end and doesn't go anywhere for cars

On the right is a wildfowl "sanctuary". This is a place where injured
birds can live, because they might not be able to look after themselves in the wild. You should be able to see or at least hear dozens of
ducks, geese and other water birds around a pond, carefully surrounded
by wire fencing to keep them safe from wild animals. Ducks and geese
can fly or swim. They can even swim underwater. Their feathers are
coated in a sort of natural oil, which keeps them warm and "waterproof".

4. **The lane heads uphill between occasional farm buildings. Avoid the signed footpath to the right, (about a third of a mile from the main**

road) and keep straight ahead – passing the house with the small pond – continue along what becomes a grassy bridleway, signed as the Bishop Bennet Way.

☺ There are high hedges on both sides of the path. This is a bridleway, which means it is also used by horses. Look out for hoof prints in the mud. Further ahead you will probably also see deep tractor marks in the trackway, and the branches of the trees and hedges hang over and cut out some of the light. Look out for ivy growing on the tree trunks. Ivy is a climbing plant and will grow on almost anything if it stays still long enough. It has tiny suckers with which it can attach itself to trees and walls.

5.   The bridleway joins a rutted farm trackway. Keep right along this, between high hedges, leading uphill.

☺ Beneath the hedges there are sandy banks, which have many rabbit holes in them. Rabbits dig their holes under trees or hedges, because the roots help to support the roofs of their burrows and stop them falling in. There are also holes dug by badgers. These are called "setts" and are often slightly larger than rabbit holes. Badgers scrape out the soil or sand from inside and leave it piled up outside the entrance to the holes. They are "nocturnal" creatures, which means that they only usually come out at night, so it is not very likely that you will see one.

6.   Look out for a well-signed bridleway to the left, again signed for the Bishop Bennet Way. Go through the gate and continue along the track.

☺ After a short way you should pass a small pond on the left, surrounded by reeds and overhanging trees. There is also an unusual plant growing here, which likes the moist soil near ponds and lakes. It is very tall and has huge leaves like umbrellas. It is related to the "rhubarb" plant, which you might have seen in gardens or on allotments, grown for its red and green stalks which can be cooked and used in pies and crumbles.

Straight ahead there is a transmitter in a field. This acts like an aerial, and can pick up radio signals. You will be able to see it from many places along the rest of the walk, so keep a look out for it.

7. **Keep along the main track until you come to the house – turn right after the house and continue to the quiet lane.**

☺ Q: There are stables at the back of the house, so you may see some horses. Horses have long "hair" on their heads and down their necks. What is this called?

   A: A "mane". Other animals have "manes" as well, such as male lions.

8. **Bear left along the lane.**

☺ See if you can spot a house with large butterflies on its walls (ON THE RIGHT). Also, if it is summer or autumn, see if you can spot any fruit trees, such as apples, or damsons, which are small dark purple plums.

9. **Follow the lane for just under half a mile. Avoid the first two footpaths to the right.**

☺ You should soon pass a triangular sign with old people on it. Triangular road signs are usually warnings. This one warns drivers to take care as there might be old people along the lane, because on the right is an old peoples' home.

   Escape route: follow the lane for a mile. Take the footpath off to the left after Quoisley Hall, then continue from Direction 21.

10. **After Wickstead Hall take the first footpath on the right, on the bend in the lane. Follow the path downhill to a further stile. Climb the stile and continue straight ahead, leading downhill to a clearly visible stile/gate and horse jump.**

☺ This is about the half way point of the walk, and from here there are views for miles over the rich, green Cheshire countryside.

11. **Cross over and continue straight ahead – the path is less clear at first, but soon leads into a dip where there is a further gate and stile.**

☺ Down below you should be able to see some water, which is called Big Mere, and also a church tower, which is the way you are heading.

Church of Saint Michael

12. Climb the stile and follow the path towards the mixed woodland (there should be a small house on a low hill to your left). You should come to a further gate/stile. Cross over and continue ahead, now with the woods close on your right.

☺ There are many different trees in the woods on your right, including prickly hawthorns, silver birch, which get their name from their silver-white bark and tall poplars.

13. Climb the stile and follow the path ahead, now with Big Mere on your left.

☺ Here there are many reeds and waterside plants, which provide food and shelter for water insects, like dragonflies and water beetles. In spring and summer there are lots of pink and yellow flowers along the water's edge. In March look out for frog spawn, which is like a clear jelly, usually around the stems of reeds.

Inside the jelly are hundreds of eggs which will hatch into tadpoles. (Don't try and eat any. It won't taste like the jelly you are used to!)

Q: Do you know what tadpoles grow into?
A: They lose their tail, grow legs and become frogs.

14. Climb a further stile and keep with the lakeside. After the next stile bear slightly to the right, to a gate leading onto the lane. (There is also a stile at another point.)

☺ There will almost certainly be ducks and geese on the water. Big Mere is a very popular place with them. Ducks and geese "moult" in summer, which means that some of their feathers come out, so they can keep cooler in the warm weather. Look out for feathers on the grass. The feathers will grow back as the weather gets colder. Dogs and cats also moult. You may have noticed that if you stroke a dog in the summer, your hand will probably get covered in loose hairs. People don't moult in hot weather; we just wear fewer clothes!

15. Bear left and follow the lane into Marbury village.

☺ Overlooking the lake is the church of Saint Michael. Like many churches it was built on a slight hill, so it can be seen from all over the village and surrounding farm lands. On Sunday mornings when the bells were ringing the people from houses further outside the village would head along the lanes and across the fields towards the tower. It acted as a "beacon", which is why most churches have tall towers or spires.

In the village of Marbury there are some very old and some newer houses. Can you tell which are which? The village green is on the right and it has an old oak tree growing in the middle, with a circular bench built around its trunk.

Q: The village inn is close to the green. What is it called?
A: The Swan Inn

16. Continue along Wirswall Road (avoiding the right turning at the pub) passing old black and white houses.

☺ On the left are some very old wooden framed buildings. The wood used for house frames was often oak, because it is strong and long lasting.

You can see it clearly, painted black. The parts in between the wooden frame are bricks painted white. These houses are three or four hundred years old. Opposite them are some more black and white buildings, but if you look carefully you will see that these have no wooden frame, they are just brick, which has been painted to look the same as the older houses over the road.

17. Pass the modern bungalows on the left, then take the footpath on the left. Bear diagonally right to a further stile – cross over and bear diagonally left.

    Escape route: (and preferred route in this new edition due to the badly signed paths and half-hidden stiles) avoid the footpath to the left, continue ahead along the lane. At the next junction (about a third of a mile) keep straight ahead along Marbury Road and you will come back to the canal. Continue from Direction 23.)

☺ The church and lake soon come into view, and keep a look out for that transmitter you passed earlier on, up at the top of the hill.

18. Take the stile straight ahead and continue to the stile/bridge. Cross over.

19. The signs after the bridge point to paths on the left and right – ignore these and continue straight ahead – there should soon be a drainage ditch on your left. Continue to the far left corner of the field, where there is a stile almost hidden in the undergrowth. Cross over and continue straight ahead across an open field, towards a clearly visible stile and long gate.

☺ You should be able to see a large farm ahead. It has a metal haybarn, in which bales of hay are stored to keep them dry from the rain. Perhaps you will see a tractor in the fields.

20. Bear left onto the lane. Look out for the footpath in the trees on the right.

21. Follow the footpath straight ahead to a stile at the edge of the woodland. Cross the stream via the plank bridge and follow the path through the outskirts of the woods.

☺ If you keep quiet you might be able to see some rabbits or squirrels. There are rabbit holes close to the path, and there are sure to be squirrels around in the branches of the trees, but the chances are they will have heard you coming and will be keeping out of the way until you have passed.

22. Cross the stile at the end of the trees and cut across the field, bearing slightly to the right, to a stile in the hedgerow. Bear left along the lane to the canal bridge.

☺ Back to the canal now. This is the last part of the journey, just a mile to go.

23. Cross the canal and bear left after the bridge, down onto the towpath. Bear right along the towpath, so the water is on your left.

☺ On the other side of the canal there are open fields, probably some with cows in, grazing on the grass, and can you see the transmitter on the hilltop? It looks a very long way away now.

There are many plants along the side of the canal, including thistles, nettles and reeds, which you saw earlier. There are also willow trees, which have long, trailing branches. They like to grow close to water where the soil is always moist. At one time their bendy branches were used for making baskets. See if you can spot any willows.

24. After just under a mile the towpath passes under a road bridge. Immediately after bear right, uphill, back to the road and lay-by.

Big Mere and Marbury Checklist

☐ A CANAL BOAT	☐ A DUCK
☐ A DUCK'S FEATHER	☐ A FIRCONE
☐ A WHITE COTTAGE	☐ A TRACTOR
☐ A BLACK AND WHITE COW	☐ A HORSE
☐ A WALKER WITH A RUCKSACK	☐ A CHURCH TOWER
☐ A BLACK AND WHITE HOUSE	☐ A PERSON WITH A DOG

6. The Cloud, Congleton

Also known as Bosley Cloud. A small piece of National Trust land on the Cheshire/Staffordshire border. It rises dramatically from the Cheshire Plain and is visible from miles away on the northern side. One of the few heathlands in Cheshire. "Cloud", by the way, means "rocky hilltop", not one of those fluffy white things.

Starting point	From Congleton follow the A54 (signed for Buxton) out of the town. After crossing over the canal take the third right turning and follow the road uphill. Head straight across at the crossroads and the starting point is $1/2$ mile on the right, where there is a small lay-by between two driveways (SJ907634). Take care not to block the driveways. There are other lay-bys further along the lane
Distance	Short route: just under 2 miles Longer route: 4½ miles
Terrain	Some uphill stretches, but nothing severe. Paths across open heathland and dense woods. Longer route includes farm trackways and some distance along lanes
Maps	OS Landranger 118
Public Toilets	None
Refreshments	None in the vicinity
Pushchairs	Totally and absolutely unsuitable

1. From the lay-by, take the stony trackway to the right, signed as a footpath, leading uphill. Continue along the track as it

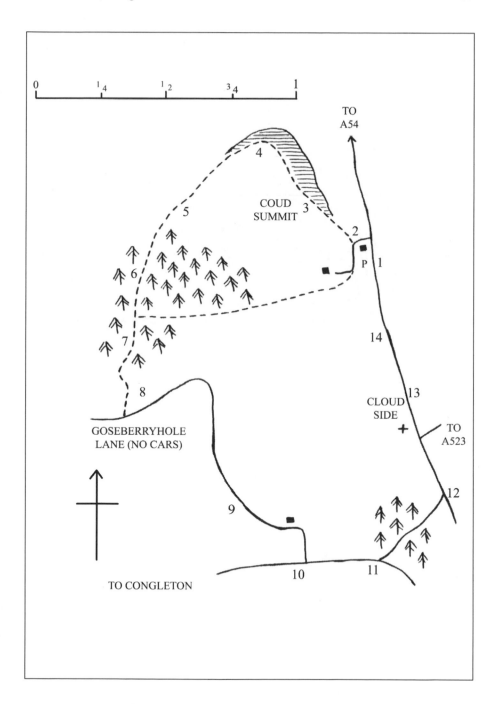

0   ¼   ½   ¾   1

TO
A54

4

COUD
SUMMIT   3

5   2

P   1

6

7

14

8   13

CLOUD
SIDE

GOSEBERRYHOLE
LANE (NO CARS)   TO
A523

12

9

10   11

TO CONGLETON

Bosley Cloud

bears around to the left. Take the steps leading steeply uphill on the right, signed for Cloud Summit.

2. **At the top of the steps, continue ahead along the well-worn pathway, towards the trig post at the summit.**

☺ To the right there are views over the surrounding countryside. The tower on the far hills is a transmitter which beams radio waves across the country. Further to the right you should be able to see Bosley Reservoir.

The path crosses moorland, with bracken and heather growing on it. Bracken is the fern-like plant which is green in the Spring and Summer but turns yellow or brown in the Autumn. Heather is dark green and grows close to the ground, where there is more protection from the strong winds. It has small flowers of white, pink or purple. There are bilberry bushes which also grow close to the ground. They have small, oval, green leaves and purple/black berries in the Autumn. Can you recognize these plants?

The sandy path climbs uphill between the heather. On the right is a cliff face and a steep drop to the fields below. Don't get too close to the edge, and remember that the wind here can be very strong!

The highest point of a hill or mountain is called the "summit". At the summit here there is a white post (Ordnance Survey Triangulation Point) which proves that it is the highest point in the area, and the highest point in the walk.

3. **Continue straight past the trig post with the "cliff edge" on your right, towards the Cheshire Plain. It is a well-worn path.**

☺ There are views over the town of Congleton and a large sand quarry. Crossing over the valley below there is a long railway bridge with many arches. This is called a "viaduct".

4. **The path continues slightly downhill, bearing around to the left, towards the woods.**

☺ There are several young trees, mainly birch, growing out of heather and bilberry bushes. They take quite a battering from the wind.

5. **Follow the path as it enters the woods.**

☺ Look for the dark, prickly gorse bushes which can have yellow lowers for most of the year. They make good shelters in which rabbits and hares can hide from passing walkers

6. **Continue through the woods, looking for a "gateway" on the right, in the corner of the woods.**

   For the longer route skip to Direction 7.

6a. **For the shorter route do not go through the gate. Instead, bear left, along a path running close to a dry-stone wall.**

☺ The trees are mainly conifers which have tall straight trunks and needle-like leaves. Most conifers are evergreens; which means they do not lose their leaves in winter. Pine, fir and spruce are all types of evergreen conifers.

Trig point

6b. Follow the path through the trees, leading slightly uphill. Keep close to the dry-stone wall at all times.

☺ Trees that lose their leaves in the winter are called "deciduous". They are more common in this country than conifers. Sycamore, oak and birch are all deciduous trees. Can you tell which trees are conifers? Look for fir cones along the path.

   Look for rabbits running away through the undergrowth of blackberries and bracken. There are many rabbit holes all over the woods. Can you see squirrels, in the treetops, or running up and down the trunks, looking for food? Over to the right there are views over the fields into Staffordshire. You may see people working on the land.

6c. At the top of the woods, take the stile in the right corner. Keep straight ahead across the field, with the drystone wall on the left.

☺ Are there cows in this field? Black and white cows are the most
    common in this area. They are called "friesians" and eat grass by
    pulling it up with their rough tongues. Cows are very nosy and may
    approach you but they are also very nervous and are probably more
    afraid of you than you are of them. In the field over the wall there
    are often horses. Both cows and horses have long tails, which they
    flick in hot weather to ward off flies.

**6d. Climb the makeshift stile on the left at the end of the field. Bear
right down the gravel driveway, leading downhill to the lay-by.
This is the end of the shorter route.**

**7. Continuation of the longer route: from the woods, go through
the gateway and follow the clear path as it leads ahead,
between bracken and brambles. It winds downhill to a rough
trackway called Goseberryhole Lane. Bear left.**

☺ The trackway is sandy and possibly muddy in wet weather. Can you
    find any horses' hoof prints or the tyre tracks of a tractor?

View across to Bosley Minn

8. **Follow the track as it bears to the right, leading slightly downhill.**

☺ To the left there are open fields and the woods of the Cloud. To the right there are views over the surrounding countryside of Staffordshire.

  Along the track there are many fine old trees, including oaks and beech. There are also many hedgerow plants. Hogweed is a tall plant with a thick, stick-like stem and many clusters of white flowers. You may see some which are taller than you. Rosebay Willow Herb is also tall, it has pink flowers at the top of a thin stem.

9. **Keep ahead, the path becomes a tarmac driveway leading gradually uphill; there should be various farm buildings visible ahead. Pass the farmhouse on the left and follow the track around to the right towards the road**

☺ In the farm garden there are fruit trees, including damsons, apples and pears. In the summer you should be able to see the ripe fruit hanging from the branches.

10. **Bear left along the lane. There are grass verges along most of this road.**

☺ If you look back to the left, you may be able to see the white stone at the summit of the Cloud, where you stood earlier in the walk.

> Q: On the right is a house built of local sandstone. It has wooden shutters at the windows. How many chimneys does it have?
>
> A: Two

☺ Over on the left you should be ale to see some large stones standing above the walls. These are called the "Bridestones" and were once part of a "burial chamber" which was like a large grave. It was built several thousands of yeas ago by one of the tribes of Stone Age people who lived in the area. The large stones form a sort of room and over the top there would have been other stones and possibly a mound of soil. The mound and many of the stones are now missing.

To visit the Bridestones, bear left along the farm driveway and go through the gate on the left to the burial chamber. Return the same way to the lane and continue.

☺ Q: What is the name of the next house on the left?
   A: The name of the house is on the gates. As it is so near to the old stones, it is also called "The Bridestones"

11. Take the left turning, along a narrow lane, cutting through trees.

☺ Feeling tired? Less than a mile to go now...

12. At the junction, bear left. Keep straight ahead. Avoid all other turnings.

☺ This is an area called Cloudside because it is close to the Cloud. See if you can spot some houses named after trees; Beech Farm

The Bridlestones

and Willow Cottage.

On the left, set back from the road, is a chapel. It doesn't have a tower or steeple but you can tell which building it is because it has all arched windows.

Q: On the left you will pass a house called "Lord's Acre". Do you know what an "acre" is?

A: It is a large measurement of land.

☺ Later there is another house called "Green Acres" and, on the right, look for the well in front of a house.

13. **Continue past a scrub field as the road begins to ascend slightly.**

☺ Q: Look for the triangular road sign at the top of the hill. It shows what looks like a "Y" upside down. Can you guess what it means?

A: It is a warning that the road gets narrower ahead.

14. **The lay-by/starting point is just ahead on the left.**

Cloud Checklist

☐ A HORSE	☐ A RESERVOIR
☐ A SAND QUARRY	☐ HEATHER
☐ AN ACORN	☐ A COW
☐ IVY	☐ FUNGUS/TOADSTOOLS
☐ A STONE WALL	☐ A TRACTOR
☐ A WELL	☐ A DOG

7. Delamere

Delamere Forest

Delamere Forest was once part of a vast hunting ground, belonging to the Norman kings, which covered most of Cheshire. There are well marked paths and trackways throughout the forest, and plenty of amenities for the family. It is still a working forest though, and areas may be closed off for felling. Certain areas may have been felled and others replanted, so allow a little leeway with the text. An ideal location for pushchairs, train travellers, naturalists and tea drinkers. If you fit into one or more of these categories, head straight for Delamere.

For info: www.forestry.gov.uk/delamerehome Delamere Forest Park: Tel. 01606 882167

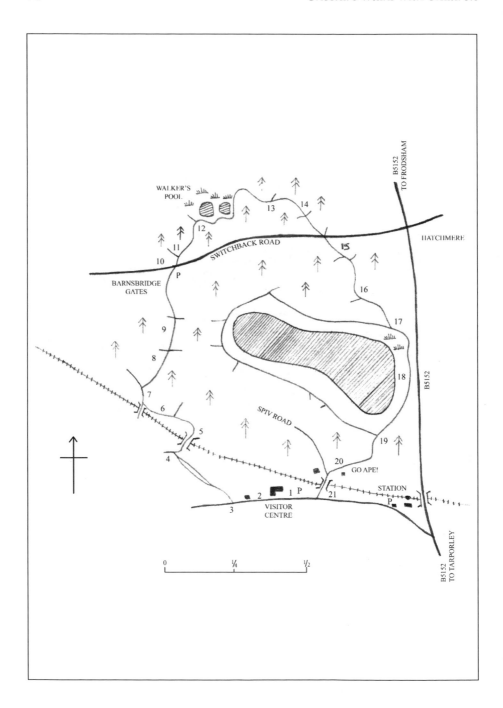

Starting point	**Delamere Forest Visitor Centre car park (SJ548704). Turn off the B5152 (Frodsham to Cotebrook road) at Delamere Station and follow the driveway to the visitor centre. There are also other car parks along this drive**
By rail	**Delamere Station, it couldn't be simpler. Trains from Chester and Manchester**
Distance	**6 miles**
Terrain	**Good forest trackways and well defined paths**
Maps	**OS Explorer 267 or Landranger 117 Delamere Forest visitors' map, available from Visitor Centre**
Public Toilets	**Visitor Centre**
Refreshments	**Café at the Visitor Centre, Delamere**
Pushchairs	**An ideal route for pushchairs. For a very short circular route park in the Barnsbridge Gates car park and follow the "Easitrail", specially designed for disabled people and pushchairs**

First call in at the Visitor Centre, which has displays, exhibitions and information relating to the forest and the area. Also there is a gift shop, refreshments and toilets. Cycle hire is also available.

1. From the Visitor Centre car park bear right along the driveway, passing the Visitor Centre on your right, then a house of painted brick.

☺ Q: In what year was this house built?
   A: 1906. There is a plaque bearing the date over the door

2. **Follow the footpath alongside the forest roadway.**

☺ Many wild plants grow alongside the track, including blackberries, wild raspberries and nettles.

> Q: If you get stung by a nettle, you can rub the sting with a certain leaf to stop it hurting. What type of leaf?
> A: A dock leaf. They are quite large and oval, and can usually be found growing next to nettles. Can you see any?

3. **Bear right along the wide footpath, leading further into the forest.**

☺ You will pass many conifers on your walk today. Conifers are trees which carry their seeds in cones – fir cones, pine cones; they have dark green needles instead of leaves. They are grown in this country mainly for their wood. Pine is particularly popular for making furniture.

Amongst the other trees are occasional rowans, which are easy to spot in the summer or autumn because of the bright orange or red berries.

4. **The path divides to form upper and lower, running parallel - take either, as they rejoin after a short way. The path winds downhill between ferns and brambles. At the junction bear right and cross the bridge.**

☺ On the right, just before the bridge is an area of beech trees. See if you can recognise them. Beech trees can live for well over 200 years, so these trees might have been here longer than the railway that passes under the sandstone bridge, possibly longer than all but the very oldest houses in the area, and certainly much, much longer than the visitor Centre.

Beeches, along with many other trees like oak and sycamore, are called "broad leaved trees" because their leaves are wide and flat, unlike the needles of conifers. They are native to this country, which means they grow here naturally, unlike most conifers, which come from abroad and are planted here by Man. Look at the trees as you pass them. See if you can tell which are conifers and which are broad-leaved.

Q: After the bridge there are many Silver Birches on both sides of the path. They have narrow trunks with silver-white bark. Do you think they are conifers or broad-leaved trees?
A: Broad-leaved.

5. Avoid any minor paths on either side, keep with the wide gravel trackway. At the major junction bear left.

☺ Different wood is used for making different things. A special willow is grown for making cricket bats. Sycamore is used for kitchenware, like cutting boards and wooden spoons. Horse chestnut is often used for making wooden toys. How many things can you name in your own home that are made of wood?

6. Follow the path as it leads downhill and runs parallel with the railway. At the junction (with the bridge on your left) bear right.

☺ There are many wild mushrooms and toadstools growing in the forest – some types can be very poisonous, especially one called Fly Agaric, which often grows under birch trees and has a bright red "cap" with white spots on it, so if you see any never touch them.

7. Keep ahead (the right hand path) at the next junction.

☺ On your walk through the forest you may come across areas that have been FELLED, or cleared of trees and you will probably find stacks of logs waiting to be taken away to factories. If you do, look at one of the round ends of the logs and see how many rings you can count. There should be a ring for each year. You will probably find the trees were twenty or thirty years old before they were felled.
   You will also come across areas that have been newly planted with young trees. These will be allowed to grow for many years and will provide wood for the future.

8. Go straight across at the crossroads and continue ahead, keeping to the main trackway and avoiding all paths on either side.

Escape route: at the crossroads bear right. Keep to the main path which will lead you in just over 1 mile to a bridge over the railway. For the car park bear right along the lane after the bridge.

☺ On either side of the path there are some very tall conifers and some equally tall sweet chestnut trees. Though these trees are very tall, their roots will probably not go very far down into the ground (usually less than 8 feet) but will spread over a very wide area, often as large as a football pitch.

Conifers are very fast growing, which is one reason why they are grown for wood. Sweet chestnuts are slower growing, but can live for over 400 years. Even older than beech trees. That may seem like a long time, but the oldest trees in the world can be found in Canada and America, and are over six thousand years old.

9. Keep to the main path which leads to a road.

Just before the road, steps on the right lead down into the Barnsbridge Gates car park, the start of the "Easitrail" for disabled people and pushchairs. There is also a notice board showing pictures of some of the many birds that frequent the forest.

10. Take great care crossing over and follow the track through the forest opposite, signed for the Sandstone Trail/Frodsham.

☺ Q: Look out for a stone "mile stone" on the right. How far is Frodsham?
   A: 12 kilometres

11. At the fork bear right through conifers along the main path. (Stick to the major gravel trackways - avoid all other minor paths leading into the trees.)

☺ Amongst the tall conifers you may see many silver birch trees; you can spot them because of their silver-white bark. Their seeds grow very easily and they can take over whole areas very quickly. There are also more rowans on both sides, with their red berries.

12. At the next junction keep right, soon passing Walker's Pool on your left.

☺ After some way, look out for Walker's Pool, through the trees to your left. It is one of the many small ponds within the forest. It is quite marshy and wet in this area. At one time the whole of the forest was like this, but most of it has dried out now. Hopefully, if you stick to the paths, you won't even need your wellies on.

13. Keep right after Walker's Pool – the track now begins to bear back round towards the road.

☺ All plants need light to live. Where the forest trees are growing very close together, no sunlight can reach the forest floor, so no plants can grow, there are only dry, dead needles covering the ground. Here the trees are not too close to cut out all the light and there are many ferns, blackberries and other plants growing beneath the trees. This jungle of greenery is called "undergrowth".

14. Keep straight ahead at the crossroads which leads back to the road. Cross over and take the trackway opposite.

☺ There are many broad-leaved trees now; sweet chestnut, beech and rowan. Later on the trees are mainly conifers.

Quiet trackway, Delamere Forest

15. Keep to the main trackway, avoiding paths to either side.

☺ If you have a real Christmas tree at Christmas, you might recognise it as a conifer. It is an ever-green, keeping its colour all the year round. The needle-like leaves do not stay on the tree forever, they drop off slowly throughout the year and new leaves grow all the time, so the tree is never bare.

16. Avoid a track to the right and continue ahead. After a short way take the wide sandy path leading downhill on the left.

☺ Acid rain is a problem which affects forests all over Europe. The fumes from cars and factories rise into the sky and mix with the clouds, so that when it rains the rainwater is acid. This damages the leaves of trees and whole forests have died. Thankfully the problem does not affect Delamere Forest, but hopefully in the near future pollution will be controlled and acid rain will no longer be a threat to the countryside.

17. Avoid a further track leading off to the right and continue ahead, now with Blakemere Moss (wetland area) on your right.

☺ The water on your right is called Blakemere Moss; it is an area of "wetland" where water-loving plants and mosses grow. Wetlands are becoming quite rare in Britain, so this part of the forest was cleared of trees and flooded in 1998.

18. Keep to the clear path running alongside the edge of Blakemere Moss. At the next major junction bear right, keeping with the edge of the water.

☺ There are many animals and birds living at Delamere. This is a quiet path, through the heart of the forest, and it is here that you are most likely to see the wildlife. Rabbits, squirrels, foxes and badgers all live in the area. The forest is also the home of many different types of birds, such as cuckoos, swallows, owls and woodpeckers.

19. The track crosses over a drainage ditch, after which there is another junction – here bear left, leading away from the water. The track winds through the trees. Keep to the main track.

Blakemere Moss

☺ There are still conifers on both sides of the path. Keep a look out for bilberries growing beneath the trees. They are low plants, which have purple berries in the summer and autumn. These berries are not dangerous to eat, though you should never eat any wild fruit without asking an adult, as many might be poisonous.

Go Ape! Around this area you will probably see ropes and walkways linking the treetops – this is part of Go Ape, a treetop adventure.

20. **Pass the Go Ape cabin on your left. Continue ahead, slightly uphill, to join the major forest roadway. Bear left towards the railway bridge.**

☺ Q: At the bridge there is a triangular sign with what looks like lightning on it. What do you think this means?

A: It is a warning that the wires ahead contain electricity and
      are very dangerous. You may see other road signs on your way
      home. Triangular ones like this are warnings, look out for signs
      that mean old people crossing, roundabout ahead or sharp
      bends in the road.

21. **Cross the railway bridge. Bear right for the car park and Visitor
    Centre.**

Delamere Checklist

☐	**A STONE BRIDGE**	☐	**BLACKBERRIES**
☐	**A COW**	☐	**A TRAIN**
☐	**A WHITE CAR**	☐	**A SQUIRREL**
☐	**A CONIFER/EVERGREEN TREE**	☐	**A SILVER BIRCH TREE**
☐	**SOMEONE WITH A DOG**	☐	**A CYCLE**
☐	**A PILE OF LOGS**	☐	**NEWLY PLANTED TREES**

8. Dunham Massey and Little Bollington

Dunham Massey Hall was originally built in Tudor times, and was renowned as one of the finest halls in Cheshire. The Victorian novelist and biographer, Elizabeth Gaskell, referred to Dunham Massey as the "favourite resort of the Manchester workpeople". Today, little has changed in that respect. The Hall, its gardens and parkland are now owned and preserved by the National Trust. Fallow deer roam freely throughout the park and the various small pools attract a wealth of birdlife. The facilities in the Stables provide for every need with a restaurant/cafe, gift shop, toilets and often free displays. The grounds are entirely flat and everything can be found in a relatively short space. Dunham Massey is one of those places, like Tatton or Lyme that is ideally suited for families.

For info: www.nationaltrust.org.uk put Dunham Massey in the search box. Dunham Massey tel: 0161 929 7508

Dunham Massey Hall

Starting point	The main NT car park on Woodhouse Lane (SJ733875) well signed from all directions
By bus	Services from Altrincham and Warrington, stops close to both starting points
By rail	Nearest stations: Hale or Altrincham
Distance	Entire route: 3 miles
Terrain	Flat parkland, canal towpath, pavement through Dunham town
Maps	OS Landranger 109
Public Toilets	The Stables, Dunham Massey Park, including disabled toilets and baby changing facilities
Refreshments	Stables Restaurant, Dunham Massey, plus a couple of country pubs en route
Pushchairs	The entire park is ideal for pushchairs, though all entrances except via the main car park have step stiles. With some degree of effort, the whole route can be managed with a pushchair, but some lifting over stiles etc will be necessary and take care along the narrower parts of the canal towpath

1. Cross the main car park to the National Trust information hut and follow the concrete path to the left, signed for the hall. Bear right and follow the path along the side of the lake.

☺ There are usually many different types of water birds on the lake, including mallards (common ducks), swans, white geese, Canada geese (with black necks), moorhens (small and black with a red stripe on their heads) and coots (small and black with a white stripe on their heads). See how many you can spot.

2. Go through the gate and continue ahead, then bear left across the moat. Go through the archway into the cobbled courtyard.

3. Continue straight ahead to the fountain in front of the hall.

☺ This is Dunham-Massey Hall. At one time there was a castle where the house now stands, but today little remains of this. The Hall was rebuilt over 250 years ago and was given to the National Trust in 1976 by the 10th Earl of Stamford, who was the last person to live here.

4. Retrace your steps back to the cobbled courtyard.

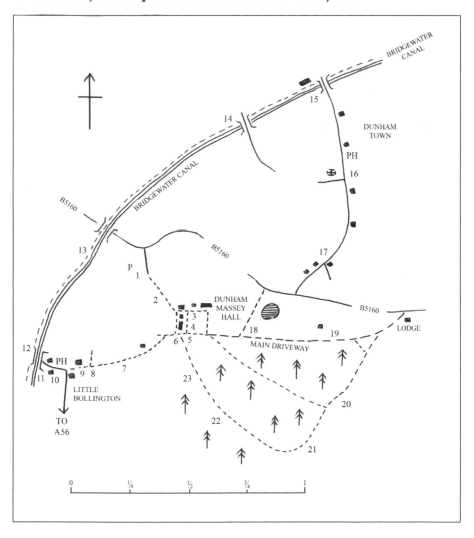

☺ Q: These buildings were once the stables, where the horses lived.
        On the roof there is a clock tower. What date is on the clock?
    A: 1721

5. **Bear left and follow the cobbled pathway, with the various stable
    buildings on your right.**

    *In the stable block there are toilets, Stables Restaurant and National
    Trust gift shop. The lower stables are often open to walk through
    (free of charge) and still contain stalls where animals were kept.*

☺ At each end of the stable block there are steps, so that ladies could
    climb up to mount their horses. On the outside walls of the stables
    there are hooks and rings where the horses' reins could be tied.

6. **Continue ahead after the stable block, then take the second right,
    passing the old mill on your right.**

The impressive front of Dunham Massey Hall

☺ This building is Dunham Mill, where corn was ground to make bread for the whole estate. Through metal bars in the wall you can see a (restored) waterwheel, which would have turned the large stone wheels which ground the corn. You can see old millstones leaning against the mill walls.

7. **Continue ahead to the step stile. Cross over and follow the path between fields.**

☺ The tall building ahead is Bollington Mill which is 150 years old. It has now been made into luxury flats. A small stream, choked with reeds and waterside plants, passes through an archway beneath the Mill.

8. **Keep straight ahead and pass Bollington Mill, crossing the narrow metal bridge into Little Bollington.**

☺ The river you have just crossed is the Bollin, from which the village of Little Bollington ahead takes its name.

    Q: What is the name of the first white house on the left after the bridge?
    A: The Mill House

9. **Continue up the lane, take care of any traffic. Pass the "Swan with Two Nicks" pub on your right.**

☺ Q: What bird is painted on the sign of the pub ahead?
    A: A swan

There are seats outside the pub, and children are welcome.

10. **Keep right, passing a black and white thatched cottage.**

11. **Follow the cobbled lane and pass under the canal bridge.**

☺ This bridge is called Bollington Under Bridge. It doesn't go under a road or railway, but a canal. If you can hear water dripping down under the bridge, don't worry. It will probably survive another few hundred years yet.

Morning mist on the Bridgewater Canal

12. **Take the narrow path to the right immediately after the bridge, which ascends to the canal. Bear left along the towpath.**

☺ This is the Bridgewater Canal. Canals are man-made, unlike rivers, which are natural. Most canals were built to carry goods, such as coal, salt or food. Today roads are used instead and the canals are used for pleasure boats only.

On the right, over the fields, you should be able to see Dunham Massey Hall, where you have just come from.

This path along the canal is called a towpath because at one time horses would walk along here pulling or "towing" the canal boats. At various places along the towpath you may see thistles, nettles and blackberries growing close to the water.

13. **Continue along the towpath. Soon the main Dunham road passes beneath you. The canal and towpath narrow here so take care.**

Escape route: to return to the park go down to the road and bear right. The main park gates are in a short way on the right.

14. Ahead you should see Dunham Town Bridge. Go under the bridge and continue.

☺ You will probably see several houseboats along the canal. These are called narrowboats because they are long and narrow. They are often painted in bright colours and decorated with flowers.

15. Directly before the next bridge keep left alongside the fence, along a narrow footpath which rises from the canal to road level. Bear right, crossing the bridge and continue along the lane, via the pavement on the left.

☺ This is the village of Dunham Town. On the left is the Village Hall, built for meetings and get-togethers. Next door is the old Schoolhouse where the children of the village were taught the basics of reading and writing. It is now someone's home. This road is named after the Schoolhouse; School Lane.

   Q: When was the schoolhouse built?
   A: There is a plaque over the door showing the date. 1759

Further along, also on the left is the "Axe and Cleaver" pub, with tables outside.

☺ The Church of Saint Mark's was built in 1864 - it has a small spire in the middle of the roof.

On the left is Dunham Town Store, formerly the Post Office.

16. Continue ahead along School Lane.

☺ Notice how many of the cottages along this lane are very similar and are painted in the same colour. These were once estate cottages where the workers at the hall would have lived, or which could be rented from the Lord of the Manor. To save money, many villagers would grow at least some of their own vegetables in their small gardens, or on allotments nearby.

17. Avoid the turning to the left and continue straight ahead through the village to the main road. Bear right, carefully cross the road

and climb the ladder stile back into the parkland. Follow the driveway ahead.

☺ On the left is Smithy Pond where there are often ducks and water birds. Along the drive the National Trust have planted a new row of lime trees to form an attractive "avenue". Old paintings show there were many avenues all over the parkland at one time, but over the years many of the trees have died and not been replaced.

18. At the junction bear left and continue along the main driveway.

Escape route: bear right instead which will return you to the Hall/stables and toilets. From the front of the Hall continue from Direction 24.

☺ Here there is an avenue of oak trees. You may notice there are some tree stumps where old trees have died or have become unsafe and had to be cut down. New trees have been planted to replace them. Very young trees will be protected, often by wooden fencing, from the deer, as there is nothing they like to eat better than the bark of young trees.

Q: What is a young tree called?
A: A sapling

Further along the drive the trees forming the avenue are beeches. See if you can tell the difference.
The building over on the left with arches around the outside is the deerhouse. It was built over two hundred years ago as a shelter for the deer. It is still in use today.

19. As the carriage drive bears left towards the gates and lodge, keep ahead/right along a wide grassy trackway. Bear right at the end along the clear sandy path.

☺ You will almost certainly see some deer along these paths. Deer are shy creatures. Do not approach them, or feed them, and do not go into the fenced off areas.

20. Go through the two gates into the deer enclosure. Continue ahead along the clear path.

Dunham Deer

☺ On the left is the boundary wall, which marked the edge of the parkland belonging to the hall. After a short way notice the railings set in the wall. This was to allow a good view from the hall, which you can see along the "avenue" of trees on your right.

21. **Go through the next set of double gates and turn right, along a wide grassy avenue between the areas of woodland.**

☺ Keep a look out for wild animals. Apart from the deer you might be lucky enough to see rabbits, foxes or even badgers. Badgers are nocturnal which means they only usually come out at night, but they can sometimes be seen after sunset. They live in long tunnels called setts. You can tell a badger sett from the hole of other animals, because they usually have heaps of soil piled outside that the badgers have scraped out with their strong paws.

22. **Continue ahead towards the Hall.**

☺ (AT THE POND TOWARDS THE HALL) The pond is surrounded by rushes and reeds, and in summer is covered with water lilies. Here you may find many of the water birds you may have seen earlier, and sometimes herons, (which have long legs).

23. Continue ahead, crossing the main drive and returning to the fountain in front of the Hall.

24. Bear left, crossing the cobbled courtyard. Go through the archway, cross the moat and bear right.

25. Go through the gates and follow the lakeside path back to the main car park.

Dunham Massey and Little Bollington Checklist

☐ A DEER		☐ A STONE LION
☐ A CANAL BOAT		☐ A RABBIT
☐ AN OAK TREE		☐ A BLACK AND WHITE COW
☐ A FOUNTAIN		☐ A WATERWHEEL
☐ A BRICK BRIDGE		☐ A POST OFFICE
☐ A STONE WHEEL		☐ A DOG

9. Great Barrow

Great Barrow is a small village a few miles east of Chester, in the midst of a rich, rural landscape, with many interesting and well-signed footpaths. The village itself is a "living village", but is a treasure-trove of quaint and odd features.

Starting point	**Bus stop/parking lay-by on the B5132, Great Barrow (SJ469684) – not far from the church**
By bus	**Services from Chester. Bus stop on the main road**
Distance	**2 miles**
Terrain	**Flat walk along field-edge footpaths, country lanes and village streets. No uphill stretches**
Maps	**OS Explorer 266 or Landranger 117**
Public Toilets	**None**
Refreshments	**Pubs only**
Pushchairs	**Around village only – follow first Escape Route**

1. From the starting point lay-by on the main village street - take the un-named lane to the right of the row of houses, signed for Saint Bartholomew's Church. At the church climb the steps and bear to the right around the tower.

☺ This is the Church of Saint Bartholomew. The sandstone tower was built over 250 years ago though the rest of the church is older.

   Q: What shape is the stained/coloured glass window in the church tower?
   A: Round.

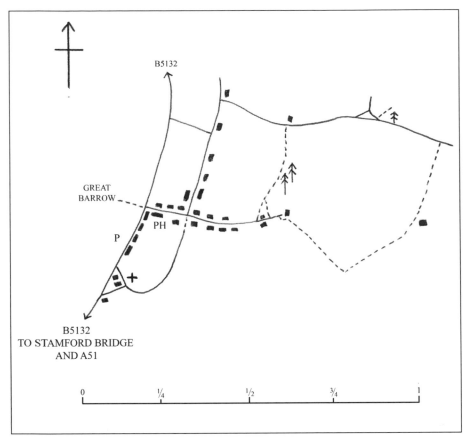

2. **Bear right along the central path between the graves to the gate. Go through the gate and bear left along the grassy trackway.**

☺ Look back at the tower. Can you see on the top of it there is a white flag pole, which might have a flag flying from it. There is also a weathervane, which shows which way the wind is blowing.

3. **Just after the churchyard bear left through a wooden gate and follow the footpath along a high wall. At the lane bear right.**

   Escape route: bear left along the lane, passing the pub. Bear left again at the junction to return you to the starting point.

☺ On an island in the middle of the road is an old water pump. At one time all the villagers would have to get their water from here. The stone trough that once caught the running water now has flowers in it.

4. Continue down Mill Lane, which is signed as a dead end.

☺ The village is a mixture of old houses and quite modern ones. Can you tell which are old and which are newer? The newer houses are brick, while many, but not all, of the older houses are stone.

   Notice "Laundry Cottage" on the left. It might seem unusual to call a house this but many old villages have a cottage with this name, and as you can guess, it was once where laundry was washed.

   Q: Can you find a house named after a prickly evergreen tree?
   A: A brick house on the left - "Holly Cottage"

5. Avoid the footpath on the left and continue ahead.

   Escape route: take the footpath on the left before the road crosses the stream. Follow the clear path across the grassy field. Climb the stile onto the lane and bear left. Continue from Direction 12.

6. The lane ends in two driveways. A footpath leads along the drive on the right. (There is a pedestrian gate at the side if the main gate is closed.) Keep left along the side of the building, avoiding the tracks and gates to the right. Take the steps on the right, leading up the sandy bank and through a gate. Keep straight ahead along the edge of the field, with the hedge on your left.

☺ Q: Soon there are oak trees growing along the edge of the field. What is the "fruit" of the oak tree called?
   A: An acorn. This is the seed of the oak tree, and if planted and watered it will grow into another tree

7. At the end of the field climb the stile and cross the plank bridge over the ditch. Bear left for a short way, then cross another plank bridge and stile. Continue ahead, signed for "Hollowmoor Heath", with a farm in view directly ahead.

☺ There are often cows in these fields. Cows swish their tails to keep flies off them. If it is summer watch them and you'll see. Never walk close behind a cow or any large animal, in case you startle them and they kick out at you.

Look out for foxes on your walk. Foxes are related to dogs. Their coats are usually a reddish colour, though they are white underneath. They live to an average age of fourteen.

Church of Saint Bartholomew

8. **Just before the farm take the stile on the left next to a metal gate. Bear right and pass behind the farmhouse.**

☺ There might be a lot of mud near the stile, because there is a water trough nearby, and the cows all come here to have a drink.

Q: How many chimney pots are there on the farmhouse?
A: Eight

9. **At the corner of the field veer left to the stile in the hedge, and bear left along the driveway.**

☺ Q: What is the name of this farm?
A: "Park Hall Farm".

There should be a metal sign near the gates, with horseshoes on it. They aren't really shoes at all, not like people wear anyway. They are made of metal and stop the horse's hooves being worn away. Horseshoes are made by a "blacksmith" who makes things from iron. At one time it was quite a common job, but these days it is quite rare.

The horseshoes are fitted onto the horse's hooves by a man called a "farrier".

10. Ignore the footpath on the right near the houses. Continue along the drive to the lane, then bear left. (There are grass verges along the lane.)

☺ Over on the left you may be able to see the church again. There are more oak trees along the lane, which in the winter seem popular with large flocks of birds. Some birds "migrate" in the winter, which means they fly south to other countries where it is warmer, but some birds stay here in Britain and brave the cold weather. They need a lot of food to survive and would be very grateful for any nuts or breadcrumbs you put out for them.

11. Avoid the minor turnings to the right and the footpaths on either side. Continue along the lane.

☺ There are hedges on both sides of the lane. Many different plants make up a hedgerow. Can you recognise any of the plants in these hedges? Amongst them are hawthorns, with sharp thorns. In the spring they have colourful blossoms; white, pink or sometimes red. Brambles or blackberries have prickly stems and also have white or pink flowers in the spring. Their fruit is, of course, the blackberry, which you have probably seen many times. There is a lot of prickly holly in the hedges, which is used as a decoration at Christmas. Another prickly plant in the hedgerow, which is quite common in this part of Cheshire, is the blackthorn or sloe, which has light green leaves and blackish berries in the autumn. All these plants have "fruit" or berries, which are eaten by birds and animals.

12. At the junction bear left, signed for Stamford Bridge.

☺ Q: At the corner look out for the old house; (ON THE RIGHT) when was it built?

A: 1881 – look for the plaque with the date on it

Q: Keep a look out for the road signs; how far is Stamford Bridge from here?

A: 1¼ miles

There are many very nice, old houses along this quiet village street. Look out for old stables and farm buildings which have been converted into houses. Over on the right you should pass a football pitch; at the weekend there might be a match underway. Do you support a football team? (Is it Manchester United?)

13. **Continue back to the water pump, then follow the road around to the right, passing the pub and post office.**

☺ Q: Look out for the village pub – what is it called?
   A: The White Horse. Look for the hanging inn sign

14.   **At the crossroads bear left to return to the starting point.**

Great Barrow Checklist

☐	A HORSE	☐	A GRAVESTONE
☐	IVY ON A TREE	☐	A MOTORBIKE
☐	A TRACTOR	☐	AN ACORN
☐	A COW	☐	A HOLLY BUSH
☐	A WOODEN BRIDGE	☐	A BLACK AND WHITE HOUSE
☐	A STONE LION	☐	A WHITE GATE

10. Great Budworth and Arley

Great Budworth is a gem of a Cheshire village, centred around the church and the village inn. It was featured – some years ago – along with nearby Arley Hall in Granada TV's whodunit quiz "Cluedo", when both places were visited by a host of internationally famous stars. The countryside, despite its proximity to industrial Northwich and the constantly busy M6, is green, fertile and very attractive. A walk across the Arley estate is rewarding in any season. (This is a 6 mile walk and there are no escape routes.)

To make this a circular walk there are some unavoidable stretches along lanes – to avoid these start at the alternative starting point in Arley village (see below). Follow the directions into Great Budworth, then return the same way.

For info about Arley Hall visit www.arleyhallandgardens.com or phone 01565 777353.

George and Dragon, Great Budworth

Starting point	Great Budworth village (SJ664775) just off the A559. Well signed from Northwich. Parking along the main village street Alternatively start at Arley village walkers car park (SJ670810), head along the driveway into Arley Hall, bear right at the crossroads and follow the main driveway. Begin from Direction 22
By bus	Services from Northwich and Warrington. Bus stop just outside Great Budworth on A559
Distance	6 miles
Terrain	Mainly flat, footpaths across farmed fields. Some stretches along lanes
Maps	OS Landrangers 109 and 118. Both maps are needed to cover entire route
Public Toilets	No public toilets along the route. Toilets at George and Dragon, Great Budworth for patrons only. Nearest public toilets at Marbury Country Park, south-west of the village
Refreshments	Pub - George and Dragon, Great Budworth. Tables outside. Children welcome. Popular at meal times, even throughout the week
Pushchairs	Unsuitable. Village and lime walk only

☺ This is the village of Great Budworth. It was once owned by the local squire (a rich landowner and country gentleman) and the villagers would have had to pay him rent for their homes. Perhaps you live in a house or a flat which is rented? This village was owned by the squire who lived at nearby Arley Hall, but more about that later.

Can you find a picture of a dragon anywhere in the village? Here's a clue - the village pub is called the "George and Dragon".

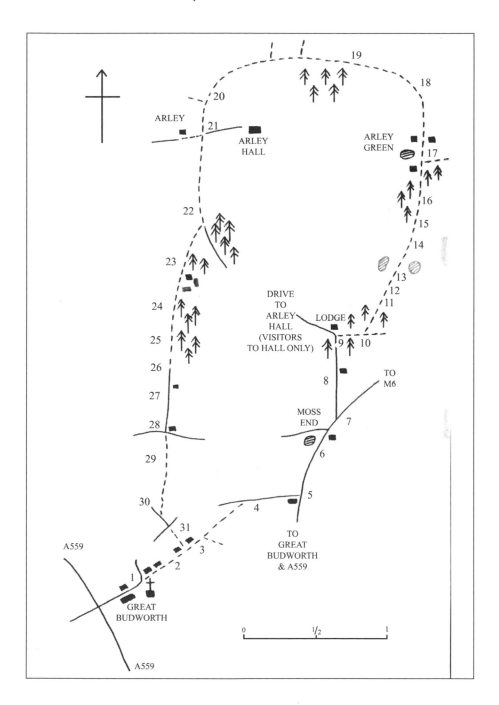

Opposite the pub is the church, made of local sandstone, with its tower which can be seen from miles away. The oldest parts of the church are nearly 700 years old, but it has been "restored" or renewed over the years.

To the right of the church gates are the old stocks, in which criminals would be imprisoned. You can see holes for the arms and head. Sometimes people would throw rotten fruit at the person in the stocks, to teach them a lesson. They were in use until 1854.

1. **Go down the narrow cobbled street, School Lane, which runs alongside the church, so the church is on your right.**

☺ The cottages along the lane are very old, mainly made of brick with thick wooden frames, which you might be able to see on some of the buildings. At the end of the lane is the village school.

2. **After the school the lane bears around to the right, but on the bend there is a footpath leading straight ahead between an avenue of lime trees. Follow the lime walk past the school field.**

☺ On the right there are views over the fields. In the distance you can probably see the smoking chimneys of Northwich, which at one time was a major salt mining town. There are several other salt mining areas in Cheshire. A place name ending in "wich" was at one time a salt mine, like Middlewich and Nantwich.

3. **Go through the gate ahead, cross over the driveway and continue along the tree lined avenue. Avoid the stile and continue straight ahead. At the end of the avenue go through the gate and bear right along the lane. (There are grass verges for much of the way.)**

Tree lined avenue

☺ Running close to the road there are a series of pylons, which carry electric cables. You will probably hear them crackling as you pass by. The electrical charge is very high, so it is very dangerous to climb a pylon. (They do little to enhance the countryside either). On the right there are more views over the countryside towards Northwich.

4. Continue along the lane towards the houses.

☺ Q: After the modern houses there is an old thatched cottage on the corner. How many chimney pots are there on the main roof?
A: Four

5. At the junction bear left signed for Arley Hall. Again there are verges for most of the way.

☺ As you pass under the wires hanging from the pylons, listen for the crackling. It will be much louder in wet weather. Along the lane there are hawthorn hedges and many other wild plants growing on the grassy banks, like blackberries and tall pink flowers called rosebay willow herb. The hedges give shelter to birds and other small wild creatures.

6. Avoid the first junction (Budworth Heath Lane) and continue ahead.

☺ On the left there is a small pond with many reeds and bulrushes around its edges, and lilies on the surface of the water. This is the first of many ponds along the walk.

Q: What is the name of the house opposite the pond?
A: Royal Oak Cottage

7. Pass a sign for Arley Hall, and take the next turning on the left.

☺ Q: Look for a sign with a "T" on it. The top part of the "T" is red. What do you think this sign means?
A: It means that for cars this road is a dead-end; it doesn't go anywhere.

After some way keep a look out for Arley Moss Farm, over on your right. If you look at the roof of the farmhouse can you see where a newer roof was added to the older farmhouse to make it bigger? Just after the farm there is another pond which has many ducks and geese on it. Apart from bulrushes around the water's edge there is also a young weeping willow tree.

8. **Continue along the lane towards the entrance lodge of Arley Hall.**

☺ Q: The small building ahead is called Willow Lodge. How many chimneys does it have?

A: Two.

Anyone wishing to visit Arley Hall can cut a chunk off the walk by bearing left along the driveway, providing the Hall is open. (Daily, except Monday in the Spring and Summer – exact times may vary. Check www.arleyhallandgardens.com for more info.) Otherwise the driveway is private. After visiting the Hall, return to the driveway and continue with Direction 22.

9. **From Willow Lodge, take the footpath off to the right, over a stile at the side of a five bar gate.**

☺ Take care, as there are many nettles along the path, and also may docks. You will probably recognise their large oval leaves, which can be rubbed onto nettle stings to stop them hurting.

10. **After a short way there is a signpost pointing left. Follow the path through the trees to a stile. Continue straight ahead across the open field, passing between the two small ponds.**

☺ There may be cows in this field, or one of the fields you walk through. If the cows are lying down it is supposed to mean it is going to rain. It is certainly true that cows lie down when there is damp in the air, but it does not always mean that there is rain on the way. Have you seen any cows lying down today? What do you think? Is it going to rain or not?

11. **At the opposite end of the field there is a plank bridge over a ditch, then a stile. Continue straight across the open field.**

☺   If there are cows in this field they will probably be black and white Friesians. Can you count how many there are?

12. Climb the stile to the left of the metal gate and continue straight across the field.

☺ Manchester Airport is not very far from here, so you may see many planes overhead as you cross the fields. Also keep a look out for tractors at work ploughing or collecting crops.

13. Again cross the bridge over the ditch and keep straight ahead.

☺ There is another pond close to the stile, and there are woods on both sides in the distance. You can probably hear the sound of cars on the motorway, which runs close by, beyond the trees.

14. Climb the stile and keep straight ahead, following the fence and row of oak trees.

☺ These trees along the edge of the field are oaks. In the late summer you should be able to see clusters of acorns at the ends of the branches. In the autumn these will fall to the ground, and some may start growing into new trees. Unfortunately, they won't last long here, because the young shoots will get ploughed up when the farmer next ploughs the field.

15. After the next stile keep ahead, with the woods on your left.

☺ This is a mixed wood which means it has lots of different types of trees growing in it. Look for rabbit holes at the edge of the woods, and keep your eyes open for them running for cover across the field. You can often see a flash of their white tails as they run away. This warns other rabbits that there is danger; that there are people or other animals coming.

16. Continue towards the brick house and climb the stile to the left of the metal gate. Continue straight ahead along the drive, passing the house on the left. At the junction a signpost indicates that there are several footpaths in all directions. Keep ahead towards the pond.

☺ Here is yet another pond. This one is quite large and has an island in the middle. Are there any ducks or geese on the water, or resting on the banks?

17. Continue along the drive, crossing Arley Brook and heading towards the buildings at Arley Green.

☺ After the pond there are houses on both sides of the path. On the left is an old black and white building which is built on sandstone blocks, which you can see at the bottom. This was at one time an old barn, but the squire from Arley Hall had it made into a school for his "tenants", or the people who rented his cottages from him.

> Q: The newer building next to it has many tall square chimneys.
>   How many chimneys are there on the main roof?
> A: Thirteen

On the right of the path there is an old water pump, and in a brick pillar behind is an old post box, from when Queen Victoria was on the throne. It is well over 100 years old. Victoria was the longest serving of all the kings and queens and was on the throne from 1837 to 1901.

18. Continue along the driveway.

☺ After a short way, you should be able to see Arley Hall over the fields on the left. The hall was the home of the squire and his family. It was built over 160 years ago. The bricks were made here, with clay dug from the ground close by. Parts of the hall had to be demolished nearly thirty years ago, when they became unsafe, and it would have been too expensive to repair them.

19. Avoid all footpaths and continue along the drive, which soon curves to the left.

☺ In case you're getting tired, you're now half way around the walk, and the next half is easier.

20. The drive soon leads past farm buildings on the left and comes to a crossroads.

☺ (AT THE CROSSROADS) On the left there is a wooden sign which points back the way you have just come. On the sign there is a rhyme:

> "No cartway save on sufferance, here
> For horse and foot the road is clear
> To Lymm High Legh Hoo Green & Mere"

Which means that the road is not for vehicles and should only be used by horses and people. The last line is a list of places nearby that the path leads to. Perhaps you have heard of some of them. The rhyme was written by the squire who had the present hall built. His name was Rowland Egerton-Warburton, and he was known as "The Rhyming Poet of Arley".

Anyone wishing to visit the Hall bear left at the crossroads. It is a very attractive house with good grounds, but not recommended for very young children.

21. Go straight across at the crossroads, pass the car parks and continue along the main driveway.

☺ On the left is the parkland belonging to the hall. There are many fine old trees, like oaks and beeches, and often cows grazing.

22. After some way along the drive bear to the left along a wide trackway, signed as a footpath. There should be open farmed fields on your right.

☺ These fields often grow crops such as wheat, corn or potatoes. If there is a crop in the field see if you can tell what it is. Wheat is yellow and grass-like. At the end of the stalks there are small grains which are ground to make flour, which is then used to make bread. The crops are collected or "harvested" in the late summer or early autumn.
   There is a great deal of wheat grown in Cheshire, and the county "coat of arms"/badge/symbol has three sheaves of wheat on it. A "sheaf" is a bundle, tied together in the middle. A common name for country pubs throughout the county is "the Wheat Sheaf".
   Once the wheat is "harvested", short stalks are left sticking out of the ground. This is called "stubble" and the easiest way to get rid of it is to burn it. Afterwards the field will be ploughed ready for next year, or might be sown with grass seed.

23. **Pass the houses on the left and continue ahead to the stile. Cross over and continue straight ahead along the footpath.**

☺ There may be cows or sheep in these fields. There are also many rabbits. Perhaps you can see some of their holes close to the hedge. Rabbits often dig their "burrows" under trees or hedges, because the roots help to stop them collapsing.

24. **Keep ahead and go through the gate at the end of the field, and follow the winding path through the woods. Cross the stream by one of the two bridges and follow the path to the left.**

☺ This is Arley Brook, the same stream that you passed earlier near the pond. The water is very clear, and the bottom of the stream is sandy. There are plants hanging over into the water, which make shelter for small water creatures. Can you see any creatures in the water, like fish, snails or water beetles?

25. **Climb the stile and keep to the left of the field, close to the hedge.**

☺ Again, these fields are often used for food crops. Potatoes have thick green leaves and grow close to the soil. The actual potatoes do not grow on the plant like apples would grow on a tree. They grow under the soil on the roots of the plant.

    Corn grows very high. If there is corn in a field and it is fully grown, you will not be able to see over it.

26. **Take the stile ahead and continue along the concrete driveway.**

☺ The hedges on either side of the drive are made up of many wild plants, some have flowers or colourful berries, like hawthorn and rosehips. These hedges and the thick "undergrowth" provide food and shelter for animals, birds and insects. Do not step off the driveway as there is a ditch on each side, which you may not be able to see because of all the plants.

    In the distance you should be able to see the pylons that you passed earlier, near the start of the walk. In case you're getting tired, there isn't much further to go now. (Just over a mile)

27. Pass the house and continue along the drive.

☺ Q: What is the name of the house on the left?
   A: Crabtree Cottage

28. At the end of the drive cross the lane and take the footpath opposite. Keep straight ahead, close to the fence on the right.

☺ These fields often have cows in them. You should pass a large water trough for the cows to drink from. Further along the field the church tower in the village of Great Budworth should come into view.

29. Climb the stile, continue ahead to a further stile, cross over then follow the path to the left, which leads around the edge of the field, soon bearing around to the right, leading slightly downhill, passing under the pylons.

☺ You should have a clear view over the village. There are some modern houses and many older ones, including some black and white cottages which have thatched roofs.
   Again, when you pass under the pylons you will probably hear the loud crackling of electricity.

30. Go through the gate in the bottom corner of the field. Take the steps that lead down to a narrow lane. Bear left.

☺ Almost there now...

31. At the junction head straight across along a trackway, then bear right at the end, following the tree-lined footpath back to the village centre.

Alternatively bear right along the lane and follow the road around to the left which comes out facing the church.

Other places of interest in the area

Marbury Country Park
South-west of GreatBudworth. Pass through Cmberbach and it is on the left.

Further walks, bird-watching, picnic area, toilets
(for more information see Marbury Country Park route)

Great Budworth and Arley Checklist

☐ A CHURCH TOWER		☐ A DRAGON
☐ A HORSE		☐ A TELEPHONE BOX
☐ A TRACTOR		☐ A POST BOX
☐ A BLACK AND WHITE COW		☐ A DUCK'S FEATHER
☐ A WATER PUMP		☐ AN OAK TREE
☐ A RHYME ON A WOODEN SIGN		☐ A PHEASANT

11. Little Budworth

Little Budworth is miles from its "great" namesake, near Northwich, but both are picturesque villages with a church, an inn and a country park close by. Little Budworth Common is several square miles of heathland with some very attractive countryside surrounding it. There are a wealth of footpaths and bridleways criss-crossing the area.

Starting point	**Little Budworth Common car park, on Coach Road (SJ591655). From Tarporley Road (A49) take the road opposite the Jardinerie Garden Centre. This is a long, straight road, and the car park can be found on the left towards the end.** **NB: car park has a height barrier of 7' 6"**
Distance	**3 miles**
Terrain	**A relatively flat circuit across Little Budworth Common and sandy bridleways**
Maps	**OS Landrangers 117**
Public Toilets	**In the car park, including disabled facilities**
Refreshments	**Pubs in Little Budworth Village. Cafe at Jardinerie Garden Centre at the top of Coach Road**
Pushchairs	**The common is flat and there are many wide paths between the trees, but most are soft and sandy, making it very difficult going for pushchairs**

1. From the car park, turn left along Coach Lane towards the gates of Oulton Park.

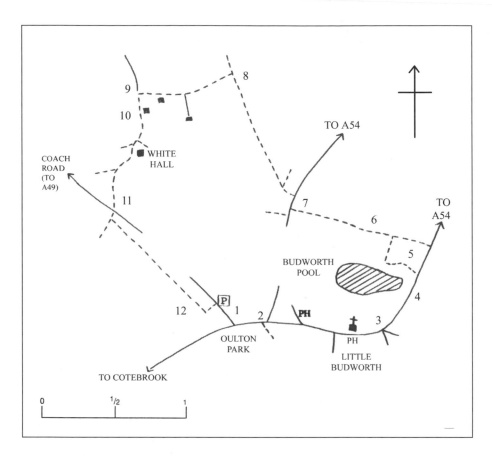

☺ The gates opposite form the ornamental entrance to Oulton Park, which is now well known as a racing track. At one time there was a large house on the site of the race track, and these were the East gates. The house burnt down in 1926. You may be able to hear the engines of racing cars. If you look through the gates you may be able to see cars going around the race track.

2. **Bear left along the lane (so the gates are over on your right), follow the road into the village of Little Budworth - pavements on both sides.**

☺ On the left is a tall cross, which is a memorial to the men from the village who died in the First World War. Just behind the cross is a pub called the "Egerton Arms", named after the wealthy family that once lived at Outlon Park.

Keep a look out in the gardens on the left, and see if you can spot a water pump, which at one time would have been used to pump water out of the ground, before running water was fitted.

Q: The village has a Church Room, which can be found on the right of this road. What is the date on the plaque on the front?

A: 1898

Next door to the Church Room is the Old Vicarage, where the vicar would at one time have lived. It is made of whitewashed brick and has a thatched roof. Next to the telephone box is the Old Post Office.

Q: What is the name of the cottage to the left of the church with roses trained along its walls?

A: Church Cottage

Saint Peter's Church and cottages, Little Budworth

This is the Church of Saint Peter. The tower is made of sandstone and is the oldest part of the church. It was built in 1526, so it's very old. The rest of the church was built over 250 years later.

Q: What is the date around the clock on the church tower?
A: 1785

3. **Follow the lane around to the left.**

☺ Q: Look out for the post box on the right. What initials can you see on the post box?
A: GR (For George Rex. Rex is Latin for King)

4. **The road winds downhill with pavement all the way. Avoid a track leading to a small mere and continue along the road, passing the edge of the water, then take the stile and follow the path through the undergrowth.**

☺ This is Budworth Pool, named after the village of Little Budworth. It has many reeds and waterside plants around its edges. In summer there are many colourful flowers here which are very popular with butterflies.

5. **The path is often used and should be easy to follow. Take the stile to the right and cut straight across an open field. Climb a further stile and continue ahead to a final stile; cross this and bear left along the sandy trackway.**

☺ There are often horses grazing in the fields next to the pool. In winter they might be wearing coats to keep them warm. Horses eat grass and hay – hay is dried grass.

6. **The track soon becomes enclosed by grassy banks and hedge-rows, then opens out with fields on either side. Continue straight ahead to the lane.**

   Escape route: bear left along the lane then right, which will take you back to Oulton Park.

7. **Bear right along the lane for a very short way, then take the**

Reed fringed Budworth Pool

trackway on the left between trees and hedges. Keep to the main trackway.

☺ This track is used for horses. Can you see any hoof prints on the ground?

8. At the fork bear left. This leads to a tarmac farm driveway. Bear right along the drive, passing paddocks and houses on the left.

☺ There are many different types of trees on either side, including sycamore and oaks. There are several rowans which have red berries in the summer and autumn. There are also many holly bushes making up the hedges, and the houses on the left have been named after them; Hollybush Bungalow and Hollybush Cottage.

9. Bear left at the junction, passing two houses on the left. The

lane then becomes a sandy trackway leading slightly downhill.
Avoid the footpath to the left and keep to the main track,
leading further downhill beneath overhanging trees. Keep left
at the junction following the wide trackway crossing a small
stream.

☺ Along the edges of the track there are blackberries and wild raspberries. Never eat wild fruit or berries without asking an adult, as they
may be poisonous. Keep a look out for fircones on the ground.

10. Pass the house on the left, after which the path rises slightly.
Pass various driveways to large houses. The drive soon
becomes flat again and bears around to the left, into the trees
of Little Budworth Common. Avoid all footpaths and continue
along the drive.

*Escape route: bear left along the signed footpath - keep straight
ahead back to the car park.*

☺ This is Little Budworth Common, once part of an ancient hunting forest
which covered most of the county of Cheshire. Today it is a HEATH
because it is covered mainly with heather, though there are now many
silver birch trees growing here, which reseed easily to make more trees.

If you look around you will probably see a silver birch. They have slim,
silvery-white trunks. Also keep a look out for mushrooms and toadstools, which can often be found on the ground where birch trees grow.
As with wild berries, never eat any mushrooms or toadstools you find
growing wild, as many types are deadly poisonous. If you like mushrooms,
it's safer to get them from a greengrocers!

11. Cross the tarmac road and continue along the path opposite,
signed for the Delamere Loop. At the crossroads of footpaths
bear left along a sandy path which runs almost parallel with
the road.

☺ Here there are many silver birches, but also look out for heather, which
grows close to the ground and has small purple, pink or white flowers.
There are also gorse bushes, which have dark, prickly leaves and yellow
flowers.

The common is the home of many wild animals, including rabbits and hares. Rabbits live in burrows in the ground, but hares, which are larger, live mainly in the middle of thick bushes, like gorse. You may hear the sound of a woodpecker, chipping away at the trunk of a tree, looking for insects.

12. Bear left and cross the road to the car park.

Little Budworth Checklist

☐ IVY ON THE WALL	☐ A CHURCH TOWER
☐ A CLOCK	☐ A WHITE COTTAGE
☐ A STONE CROSS	☐ A DOG
☐ A HORSE	☐ A TRACTOR
☐ BLACKBERRIES	☐ AN COW
☐ A RACING CAR	☐ A STREAM

12. Lyme Park and Bowstones

Lyme Park has something for everyone, a historic hall, two breeds of deer, miles of parkland, a wilderness of open moorland and panoramic views. Lyme Hall was the home of the Legh family, who have lived within the Park since the 1300s. The Park is open daily from 8 until dusk.

For info: www.nationaltrust.org.uk put Lyme Park in the search box. Lyme Park tel: 01663 762023

Starting point	The main car park, Lyme Park (SJ962823)
By rail	Nearest station – Disley. Bear left along the main road to the park gates – half a mile
By bus	Frequent buses along A6 from Stockport and Buxton directions. Ask for Lyme Park, bus stop is located close to main gates
Distance	4 miles
Terrain	Some uphill stretches on grassy moorland. Grassy paths, some gravelled
Maps	OS Landrangers 109 OS Outdoor Leisure 1
Public Toilets	Next to Park coffee shop, near mill pond. Also disabled toilets
Refreshments	Main car park, tea room at Hall, coffee shop near mill pond
Pushchairs	Most of the main parkland is accessible for pushchairs but the moorland areas are not, making this route unsuitable. The Park, however, has enough to entertain children for an entire day without having to stray far from the flat central parts

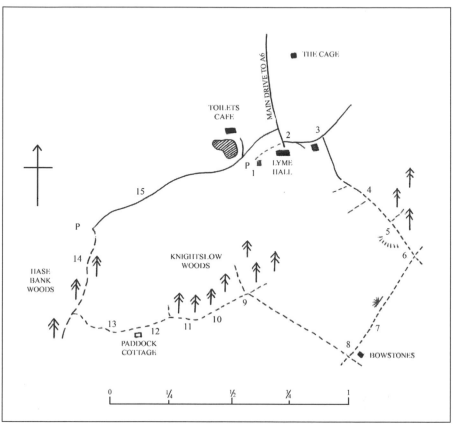

1. **Climb the steps to the left of the National Trust office, which is situated near the beginning of the main car park. At the top of the steps bear right into the courtyard of Lyme Hall.**

☺ This is Lyme Hall; the oldest parts are 400 years old, but most of it was rebuilt 200 years ago. In 1946 it was given to the National Trust, who now look after it. The hall is supposed to be haunted by a ghost called the White Lady. She has been sighted many times by visitors and staff.

2. **Return through the gates and follow the main driveway as it winds uphill. Avoid the right turnings for the stable block.**

☺ There is another grand building to the right. This was the stable block, where the horses were kept, and where the butler lived.

Q: What is on the top of the building above the archway and what is it for?

A: A weather vane, which shows which way the wind is blowing

3. **Go through the iron gate on the right immediately after the stable block and follow the driveway straight ahead to another gate. Go through this into an open meadow. Continue along the track.**

    Escape route: to return to the main car park, look out for the gate on the right which leads into the fallow deer park – it is closed between November and March. Follow the path – keeping right alongside the Hall and gardens, back to the rear of the car park.

4. **Climb the ladder stile at the end of the meadow.**

☺ The tree next to the stile is a LIME, from which Lyme Park takes its

Once a summerhouse, once a prison – the "Cage" at Lyme Park

name. There are lots of these trees all over the estate. (Limes (the fruit) don't grow on them.)

Escape route: to avoid the major uphill stretches bear right after the ladder stile, follow the clear path keeping the wall on your right. Avoid all minor gates into the woods. At the crossroads of footpaths go through the main gate into the woods, keep straight ahead which will bring you eventually back to the main car park.

5. **Follow the path uphill into open moorland, keeping the wall close on the left.**

☺ On the right towards the top of the hill is a disused quarry. Gritstone was cut from this quarry. It is a particularly strong stone, and it is believed it was used in the building of the hall.

6. **Keep uphill alongside the wall. At the top bear right, continuing along the wall. Do not cross the stile.**

☺ After some way you should come to a stone monument. This is the highest point in the park and from here there are views all over the surrounding countryside, to the hall, the cage and all over Stockport. On top of the stone monument is a disc showing the distances of all the places you can see from here.

   Q: How far is Stockport from here?
   A: 6 miles

7. **Continue along the wall, which now leads downhill. On the left are various aerials/masts, and a whitewashed farmhouse at Bowstones.**

☺ Keep a look out for Lyme's famous deer, which can often be seen in this area. They are shy and timid creatures, so do not go too near to them. There are two types of deer in the park. Red deer are large and have a reddish brown coat. Fallow deer (like Bambi) are smaller and have white spots on their backs. If you spot any deer, see if you can tell which type they are.

8. **Avoid the ladder stile on the left near the whitewashed house**

(Bowstones) – instead bear right, heading downhill on a well worn pathway.

☺ There are often herds of deer grazing on the moor here and sometimes Highland Cattle with very long horns.

9. **At the bottom of the path go through the gate into Knightslow Wood.**

   Escape route: to return to the car park, continue straight ahead along the main path, which will take you back to the main car park.

10. **Bear left in Knightslow Wood and follow the path around the perimeter of the woods, keeping the wall on the left.**

☺ A ghost story ... Look into the trees (ON THE RIGHT) and see if you can see anything moving among the shadows because these woods are supposed to be haunted ... Long ago, one of the Lords of Lyme Hall was injured at war, and was brought home to the hall, where he later died.
   According to the legend, he was buried here, on the hill beneath the trees and sometimes a ghostly funeral procession has been seen walking from the hall to these woods, carrying the body of the dead Knight. It is supposed to be his daughter, Lady Blanche, who haunts the hall and Lyme Cage, the tower on the hill.
   Apart from ghosts, keep your eyes open for squirrels and see if you can find any fir cones on the ground.

11. **Keep to the left, avoiding paths leading further into the woods, and you will come to a stile in the corner of the woods. Climb the stile, cross the stream via the stone footbridge and follow the steps downhill. Follow the path alongside the wall.**

☺ The land here is "eroding" or wearing away, partly because of the number of people who visit the park and use these footpaths. The National Trust, who own the park, have to take care of the paths (notice how the path is supported on the left by wooden planks) to make sure that they remain here for future generations.
   On the right is a wall. It is called a "drystone" wall because no

cement is used to hold it together. Many of these walls were built hundreds of years ago, but have survived because they were so well made.

12. **At the end take the path leading away from the wall and go through the gate. Climb the stony path through the trees to Paddock Cottage.**

☺ This is a small house called Paddock Cottage. It is several hundred years old, and was lived in by people who worked in the park until 60 years ago, then it became unsafe, but has recently been restored and made safe again. It is sometimes open to the public. From here there are good views over the moorland back up to the white house at Bowstones, and over the Cheshire Plain.

13. **Continue past Paddock Cottage, heading towards the Cheshire Plain, follow the grassy path leading downhill, with rhododendron bushes on the right. This soon becomes a stony and rutted trackway, winding down into Hase Bank Woods. Bear right along the driveway.**

☺ This was once one of the main drives to the hall. There are many different types of tree here, including conifers which are also called evergreens because most of them do not lose their leaves in the winter. See if you can tell which they are.

14. **Go through the gate at the top of Hase Bank Woods and follow the road to the right.**

The low hill to the left of the drive is called The Knott. Anyone who still has surplus energy can climb to the top for further views over Stockport and over the park to Lyme Cage.

☺ There are often sheep grazing in this area. See if you can find any strands of wool on the grass. Sometimes people fly kites from the hill on your left, because it catches the wind at the top.

15. **Keep ahead with the main driveway, which eventually leads back down to the main car park.**

From the main car park bear left towards the timber yard for the toilets, National Trust shop and café.

Lyme Park Checklist

☐	A JOGGER	☐	A FIR CONE
☐	A DEER	☐	A PLANE IN FLIGHT
☐	A SHEEP	☐	A BLUE CAR
☐	A SQUIRREL	☐	A WHITE DUCK FEATHER
☐	A PERSON CYCLING	☐	A BLACK AND WHITE COW
☐	A PERSON WALKING THEIR DOG	☐	A RABBIT

13. Lyme Park from Disley

Lyme Park is set in the north-east corner of Cheshire and is part of the Peak District National Park. It is run by the National Trust and is a popular weekend venue for families and serious walkers alike. The Park marks the start of many fine walks, including the Gritstone Trail, which runs for 18 miles and finishes in Staffordshire. The Park is open daily from 8 until dusk.

For info: www.nationaltrust.org.uk put Lyme Park in the search box. Lyme Park tel: 01663 762023

Starting point	Outside the Ram's Head pub, Disley. (SJ974846) parking along the lane leading to the station
By rail	Disley Station – trains from Stockport, Manchester and Buxton
By bus	Frequent buses along A6 from Stockport and Buxton directions
Distance	Just over 3 miles
Terrain	Some uphill stretches on grassy moorland. Grassy paths, some gravelled
Maps	OS Landrangers 109 OS Outdoor Leisure 1
Public Toilets	Next to Park coffee shop, near mill pond. Also disabled toilets
Refreshments	Main car park, tea room at Hall, coffee shop near mill pond
Pushchairs	Unsuitable. Much of the Park itself, however, is suitable for short walks with a pushchair and Lyme has enough to entertain children for an entire day without having to stray far from the flat central parts

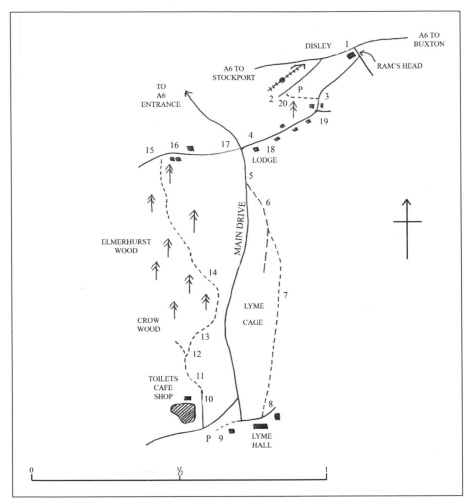

1. **With your back to the Ram's Head cross the Green and bear left along the road, passing the public toilet, then bear left along the lane towards the station, passing the children's playground.**

2. **Towards the end of the lane, opposite the station, are a set of steps next to a noticeboard about the Gritstone Trail. Climb these steps, keeping to the left, up the main steps with the handrail.**

☺ See if you can count how many steps there are.

3. **At the top of the steps bear right along the lane, leading uphill and round a tight bend. Keep right along a wide pot-holed lane, leading gradually downhill. Avoid all footpaths to either side – keep straight ahead all the way.**

☺ There are many large houses along this lane; many have big gates and big cars parked on the driveways. After the houses you should have a view to the left over fields, in which there will probably be horses. In the distance, on the top of the hill you should see what looks like a small castle – this is Lyme Cage – more about that later.

4. **The lane comes to an end at one of the lodges and gates of Lyme Park. Go through the gate and follow the roadway down to the main drive. Bear left and follow the drive.**

5. **The drive winds gently through attractive parkland. Look out**

Lyme Cage

for a clear trackway leading off to the left. Follow this as it leads uphill between oak and sycamore trees.

Escape route: to avoid the uphill section keep ahead alongside the driveway to the main car park and continue from Direction 9.

☺ Keep a look out for Lyme's famous deer, which can often be seen in this area. They are shy and timid creatures, so do not go too near to them. The males have antlers. The females don't.

Q: What do you think deer eat?
A: Leaves, young shoots and occasionally nuts, fruit and bark

There are two types of deer in the park. Red deer are large and have a reddish brown coat. Fallow deer (like Bambi) are smaller and have white spots on their backs. If you spot any deer, see if you can tell which type they are.

6. **As you gain height, Lyme Cage comes into view. Bear left along the track to the Cage.**

Escape route: to avoid the further climb to the Cage continue ahead along this old driveway – and rejoin the route at the Hall – from Direction 8.

☺ Lyme Cage was built as a "viewing house" where the family from Lyme Hall could look out over the park and the surrounding countryside. It is supposed to be haunted by a ghostly White Lady, who appeared every night to the shepherd and his family who lived there at one time. From here, take a look at the views over Cheshire, Stockport and Manchester. Perhaps you can see where you live? There are two airports in sight, (Woodford and Manchester) so you may see many planes taking off or landing.

Q: What is above the doors of the Cage and what are they used for?
A: Over each door there is a sun-dial, which is used for telling the time ... but only when the sun shines. On one side there is also an inscription; "Remember thou thy Creator in the days of thy youth".

7. **Continue past the cage on the main trackway. Keep ahead along the crest of the hill, until it drops down to Lyme Hall. Continue ahead to the courtyard in front of the Hall.**

☺ This is Lyme Hall, the largest house in Cheshire; the oldest parts are 400 years old, but most of it was rebuilt 200 years ago. The family who lived here had many houses all over the north-west, and Lyme Hall was just a sort of holiday home for them. (Rather extravagant for a holiday home if you ask me.) In 1946 Richard Legh gave it to the National Trust, who now look after it and open it to the public.

   The Hall is also supposed to be haunted by the same White Lady that haunts the Cage on the hilltop. She has been sighted many times by visitors to the Hall.

   Q: What animals guard the top of the gateposts to the hall?
   A: Stone lions

8. **Leave the courtyard the same way and bear left down the steps. At the bottom on the left is a National Trust Information Office.**

9. **Bear right across the edge of the main car park, cross the main driveway and take the roadway signed for the timber yard, which runs alongside the pond. Enter the timber yard.**

   In the timber yard there are toilets, café and National Trust shop.

☺ At one time these buildings were workshops. There was a waterwheel here which provided power for woodcutting. All the wood for the estate was cut here.

10. **Come out of the timber yard the same way and bear left, crossing the private driveway, then bearing left again along a gravelled footpath.**

☺ The houses on the left are called Chestnut Cottages. Many of the trees through these woods are Horse Chestnuts, from which conkers come. If it is late summer or autumn you might find some on the ground, but never try and knock them from the tree as this can damage it.

11. **Go through the gate into Crow Wood. Join the main pathway leading away from the timber yard buildings.**

12. **Bear right at the junction, crossing over the stream.**

☺ The water comes through a tunnel under the path. It is an overflow from the pond near the cafe. Along the banks of the stream there are ferns and reeds, and other plants that like wet ground.

13. **Continue along the path to the end of the woods. Climb the stile over the drystone wall and follow the steps uphill. Bear left along the path.**

Down below adjacent to the stream are several sewage filtration beds, just in case anyone asks.

☺ There are several beech trees along the path. In the autumn you should see many beechnuts on the ground, which squirrels like to eat.

14. **Follow the path down to a step stile into Elmerhurst Wood and follow the path down the steps and over a series of wooden footbridges.**

☺ This wood is of mixed trees, including willows along the stream. Further in the woods there is thick undergrowth, like nettles and blackberries, as well as wild flowers.

   When the trees are very close together, no light can get through to the ground, so no plants grow there. All plants need sunlight on their leaves to be able to grow. Where the trees are further apart, like here, plenty of sunshine can get through.

   Also on the ground you may see fallen trees, which have started to rot. They make homes for thousands of insects which can easily burrow into the soft, decaying wood.

15. **Climb the ladder stile and bear right – keep to the main driveway.**

☺ You will pass Northpark Cottages on the right, which will have been built for park workers.

Lyme Hall

16. Follow the driveway over two bridges, passing Brookside Cottage on the left.

☺ Q: On the left is Brookside Cottage. How many chimneys can you count on the main building?

   A: There are two on the main house, but also one on an outbuilding to the left

16. Cross straight over the main driveway and continue ahead to the lodge and gates.

17. Go through the gate and retrace your steps along the lane.

☺ There are many "evergreen" trees and plants along this lane, including prickly holly, ivy which is a climbing plant and can be found creeping up the trunks of the trees, and rhododendrons – which have large colourful flowers in the summer. See if you can spot any of these evergreens.

18. At the junction keep left, then return down the steps towards the station.

☺ Try counting the steps again and see if you get the same number as you did going up.

19. At the bottom bear right and follow the lane past the playground and back to the Ram's Head/starting point.

Lyme Park Checklist

☐	A TRAIN	☐	AN EVERGREEN TREE
☐	A HORSE	☐	A DEER
☐	A CHURCH TOWER	☐	A RED CAR
☐	A JOGGER	☐	A DUCK
☐	A PERSON CYCLING	☐	AN ACORN
☐	A PERSON WALKING THEIR DOG	☐	A HOLLY BUSH

14. Lymm Dam

A short walk perfect for a Sunday stroll, good for pushchairs, good for bird watchers. Just outside the centre of Lymm, with several nice pubs close by if you want to walk off a Sunday lunch.

Starting point	**Lymm Dam itself (SJ682869) on the A56 in Lymm**
By bus	**Services from Warrington and Altrincham – stops in sight of the dam**
Distance	**Just under 2 miles**
Terrain	**Good level paths**
Maps	**OS Landrangers 109 or Explorer 276**
Public Toilets	**Pay toilets on the east side of the dam**
Refreshments	**A pub on the east of the dam**
Pushchairs	**Good, level paths available – follow pushchair directions**

1. **With the lake on your left head to the end of the dam.**

☺ This is Lymm Dam – a dam was built to block the waters of a stream, so people could cross this valley. The earliest dam was built in 1824. There are good views from here across the water to the tower of Saint Mary's Church. The bells of the church ring every hour on the hour, so listen out for them.

2. **Take the footpath directly after the dam (avoid the steps down to the seating area) signed for Crosfield Bridge ¾ mile. Continue along the lakeside path.**

    Pushchairs/wheelchairs take the ramp on the right, signed as Easy Access, which will take you around the stepped areas. Follow the slope uphill then across a grassy area - keep ahead with the main path then continue from Direction 5.

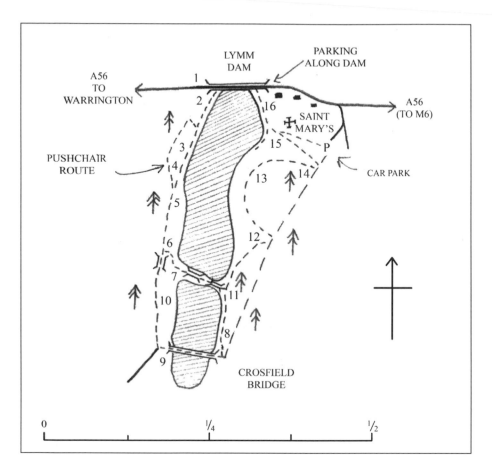

☺ The lake is popular with many water birds, including mallards, the common ducks; the males are colourful, usually with green heads; the females are brown.

Q: What is a young duck called?
A: A duckling

You may also see geese, white geese or Canada geese, which have black necks. There may also be visiting swans.

Q: What is a young swan called?
A: Not so easy this time ... It's a cygnet

3. Avoid steps to the side and keep ahead along the main path.

☺ There may sometimes be seagulls on the lake. People believe seagulls come inland when the weather is very bad at sea. You might also be lucky enough to see cormorants – which are quite large black birds – they would be likely to be standing on the bank or on logs gazing across the water. Sometimes they spread their wings out to dry them in the sun – it is a very impressive sight.

4. The path goes up three steps, then bear left.

☺ Q: The trees along this part of the lake are mainly oaks. What is the seed of the oak tree?
A: The acorn. A new oak tree would grow from an acorn. There is also prickly holly nearby

5. Keep with the main path as it bears slightly away from the lake.

Lymm Dam

☺ The path now heads through an area of tall beech trees. The seed of
   the beech tree is called a beech-nut; these have a prickly casing and
   fall to the ground in the autumn, where they will be collected by hungry
   squirrels.

   Pushchairs/wheelchairs: continue over the wooden footbridge.
   Proceed to Crosfield Bridge and cross over. On the other side take
   the left hand path signed for Church Road. Keep to the upper
   path all the way. Go through the car park and bear left along the
   road to return to the dam.

6. **Bear left from the main path before the wooden bridge,**
    signed for the Wishing Bridge. Follow the rough path
    and cross a further wooden footbridge over the stream
    then follow the path to the left. (Beware of the drop on
    the left!)

☺ A stone and metal footbridge should soon come into view ahead.
   This whole area was once the garden of a large house nearby, called
   Beechwood, which has long since fallen into disrepair and been
   demolished. This little bridge was built by the owners of the house.
   There is a waterfall flowing under the bridge, from the little pond
   into the lake.

7. **Cross over the bridge, continue ahead and cross a wooden**
    bridge over an overflow channel. Climb the steps and bear
    right, with the water on your right.

☺ Ahead you should be able to see a large concrete bridge; this is
   "Crosfield Bridge". It was built at the end of the First World War.
   That was 1914 to 1918. Can you work out how long ago that was?

8. **Climb the steps and cross over Crosfield Bridge.**

☺ There are views from the bridge, back to the Wishing Bridge. Can you
   see any ducks on the little pond below?

9. **Bear right after the bridge and follow the main path back to**
    the wooden footbridge, after which bear right, again signed
    for the Wishing Bridge.

10. **Retrace your steps over the further wooden bridge, along the path, over the Wishing Bridge, the overflow bridge and this time bear left, with the water on your left.**

☺ The archway you might see on your left on the shore of the lake was once a boathouse used by the owners of the big house nearby.

11. **Keep left and eventually climb the shallow steps and bear left along the main path.**

☺ Many wild animals live around Lymm Dam, including squirrels, rabbits, mice and foxes. If you walk quietly you never know what you might see. There are also bats here – bats are like flying mice; they are nocturnal, which means they only come out at night.

   The best time to see them is when it is just going dark. Bats fly in a figure of eight; they use a type or radar to see where they're going. They sleep in the daytime, hanging upside down.

12. **Where the path splits bear left, keeping with the lake.**

   There are benches and picnic tables in this area, and a viewpoint across the lake.

☺ From here you get a good view across the lake back towards the dam – and you can see how the dam is built. There are probably many water birds swimming across the lake. How many different types can you see?

13. **Keep left with the lake.**

☺ Soon the church of Saint Mary's should come into view with its square tower. Have you heard the bells chime yet? When they do there should be one chime for each hour, so there will be two chimes if it's two o'clock.

14. **Rejoin the main path, bearing left. Bear left down the steps, signed for Church Road. Keep ahead. Follow the partially stepped path, keeping left and pass the church over on your right.**

☺ There has been a church on this site for many hundreds or years. The present building was built in the 1850's. Can you work out how long ago that was? It is built of sandstone.

15. Follow the steps downhill then bear right along the lakeside.

☺ You might notice there is a lot of sand under your feet now – there is a sandstone outcrop up on the right. Much of the county of Cheshire is on sand. Sandstone is a reddish colour and is quite soft – as you can see on the right, it is rounded and is wearing away.

16. Keep ahead and rejoin the road, bearing left to the starting point.

The pay toilets are to the right at this point.

Lymm Dam Checklist

☐	A WHITE DUCK	☐	AN BROWN DUCK
☐	A SWAN	☐	A SQUIRREL
☐	A HORSE	☐	A COW
☐	AN ACORN	☐	A WOODEN BRIDGE
☐	A STONE BRIDGE	☐	A TREE WITH BERRIES
☐	A BIRD'S FEATHER	☐	A YELLOW FLOWER

15. Macclesfield Forest

An exhilarating walk on the border between Cheshire and Derbyshire with some fine views – some of the finest in Cheshire, and an optional walk up to Shuttlingsloe – one of the highest points in the county – well worth the extra effort on a good day.

Please bear in mind this is a working forest and some paths may be closed when trees are being felled. Also changes to the forest paths and trackways can occur. Try to get the current information leaflet from the Ranger Station before you set off.

Starting point	Trentabank car park, Macclesfield Forest (SJ961711). South west of Macclesfield, 1½ miles west of Langley
Distance	3 miles. 5 with the climb to Shuttlingsloe
Terrain	Forest trackways and footpaths, undulating, many uphill stretches
Maps	OS Landrangers 118, Explorer 268
Public Toilets	At Trentabank car park
Refreshments	Caravan in the car park at peak periods, serving all manner of food – including cake and custard!
Pushchairs	Not recommended, but passable with a sturdy "off road" type buggy and a lot of effort

There are toilets, often refreshments and a Ranger Station in the car park. A leaflet/map of the forest is usually available.

1. From the Trentabank car park return towards the road, bearing right after the rangers hut along the pathway running parallel with the road. (You should pass a picnic area on the right.)

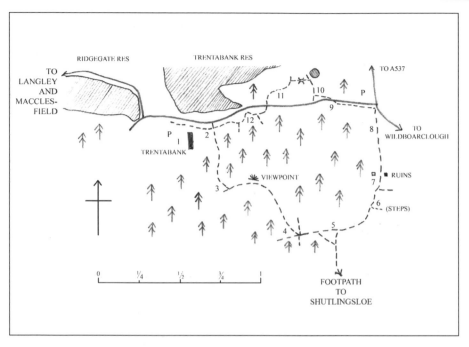

☺ Welcome to Macclesfield Forest. This is a working forest, which means
the trees are grown for their wood, so you may see areas being felled –
the trees being cut down.

Q: What is a lumberjack?
A: Someone who cuts down trees. If you see any around the forest
      – rather than wearing check shirts like they do in cartoons, they
      will probably be wearing high visibility yellow tops and hard hats
      for protection.

Most of the trees in the forest are conifers – because they grow
quickly and they grow tall and straight, so they are ideal for sawing
into long straight planks of wood.

Q: What does conifer mean?
A: A conifer is a tree which has cones – the seeds of the tree are
      contained within the cone. See if you can find a fir cone or pine
      cone on your walk. Conifers have dark green needles instead of
      flat leaves.

2. At the junction bear right along the forest trackway, leading uphill.

☺ Most – but not all – conifers are evergreens, which means they don't lose their leaves in the winter. Larches are a type of conifer that are deciduous – they lose their leaves in the winter.

If you come walking here in the winter months the forest looks much the same, with most of the trees still dark green. You may recognise some of the smaller, younger trees as Christmas trees.

Many birds live in the forest, including woodpeckers (listen for their tell-tale tapping sound as they drill the trunks of the trees with their beaks) buzzards, ravens and herons.

3. At the junction keep left along the wide trackway. Keep with the main pathway.

Macclesfield Forest with Shuttingsloe in the mist

☺ Look out for the amazing views over the forest towards the reservoirs. A reservoir is a man-made lake, usually made by building a dam across a stream. The water is then stored up and used for drinking or running factories.

The hill you might be able to see in the distance on the right is called Shuttlingsloe, and it is one of the highest points in Cheshire. It is an exciting climb to the top and there are amazing views right across the county and into Wales.

4. **Keep with the main track, avoiding all other turnings.**

   Optional extra – at the signpost bear right, signed for Shuttlingsloe, for an exciting climb to the top of one of Cheshire's highest points. The walk is mainly paved with flagstones but with some scrambling over rocks towards the end. Rewarding in good weather, well worth the effort. Return the same way.

5. **Remain with the main track, which winds and undulates through the forest.**

☺ On your way through the forest you may see trees being cut down and stacked up in piles of logs – if you do, take a look at the sawn ends of one of the logs. You should be able to tell how old a tree is by counting the rings – each year a tree grows another ring.

6. **Avoid the steps leading off to the right, continue ahead.**

☺ Animals you might see in the forest include squirrels – who eat the seeds of the trees, acorns, beech nuts and seeds from the cones - also there are mice, bats, rabbits and foxes. Foxes are related to dogs – they have reddish brown coats.

7. **The track leads between some old ruins. Continue ahead.**

☺ Notice, where the trees are very close together it is dark between their trunks and nothing grows – this is because plants need light to grow. On the ground between the trees there are usually just dry, dead needles. Where the trees are a bit further apart and light can get through there might be grass and brambles or ferns growing.

8. **Continue ahead - at the end of the track go through the gate on the left and follow the pathway downhill, with the lane over on your right.**

☺ There may be plants growing along the side of this path, including brambles (blackberries) and stinging nettles, which you will most certainly already know. Look out for dock leaves – in case you need them.

9. **At the end of the pathway cross over the lane and go through the gate opposite.**

Escape route: continue along the lane, all the way back to the car park.

10. **Follow the footpath parallel to the road, when it joins the trackway bear right. It soon comes to a small pond on the right. Bear left across the wooden footbridge. Keep left, signed for Trentabank.**

☺ Some areas in the forest are felled – cleared of trees – but in other areas new trees are planted to replace them. You may well have passed young trees on your walk. Some of these trees are used for Christmas trees. Evergreen trees are used because they keep their colours through the winter.

> Q: Three other evergreen plants are traditionally used as decorations at Christmas, can you name them?
> A: Holly, ivy and mistletoe

11. **The path drops back down to the road. Carefully cross over and join the woodland path.**

☺ Back in the woods again ... This path crosses over a stream. The stream runs into the nearby reservoir and keeps it topped up with water. The reservoir was built over a hundred years ago to supply drinking water for the nearby town of Macclesfield. There are two reservoirs in the forest.

12. **Keep right at all times. The path winds and undulates, but runs fairly close to the road at all times.**

☺ Today you've walked though a working forest, which is still used to produce wood. Wood is used for floorboards, to make furniture, fences and telegraph poles. Think about your house – how many things in it are made of wood?

13. Avoid all left turnings, keep alongside the lane.

A detour across the lane to a viewing point over the reservoir will reward you with views across the water to a heronry in the treetops. The ungainly birds can often be seen perched in the tops of the tall trees. A CCTV link showing their nests can be viewed in the Ranger Station back in the car park.

☺ Q: What is a heron?
   A: A type of bird: white with long legs, so it can stand in water

14. Continue ahead, back to Trentabank car park.

Macclesfield Forest Checklist

☐ A FIR CONE	☐ AN ACORN
☐ A WHITE CAR	☐ A DOG
☐ A HORSE	☐ A SQUIRREL
☐ SOMEONE WITH A RUCKSACK	☐ A HERON
☐ SOMEONE WITH A WALKING STICK	☐ A TREE WITH BERRIES
☐ A BLACKBERRY BUSH	☐ A FALLEN TREE

16. Marbury Country Park
(near Northwich)

Marbury Country Park was once the site of Marbury Hall, now demolished. It should not be confused with the village of Marbury, near Whitchurch. The grounds of the old Hall are now open to the public, and there are walks through woodlands, parkland and along the lake and canal. Just a stone's throw from industrial Northwich, but quite a different world.

Starting point	The car park, Marbury Country Park. (SJ652763) go along the drive and take the first left turning into the car park. Marbury can be found between the A533 and A559 just outside Northwich, and is well signed
By rail	Nearest station - Northwich 1½ miles away. Bus service available to complete the journey. From Lostock Gralam Station it is possible to walk almost all the way along the canal (2 miles)
By bus	Services from Northwich and Warrington. Stops close to the park entrance
Distance	2 ½ miles
Terrain	Mainly flat paths, mostly gravelled across parkland and through woods
Maps	OS Landrangers 118
Public Toilets	In the park, including disabled facilities
Refreshments	None on site. Pubs at nearby villages of Comberbach and Great Budworth. Pubs, cafes and restaurants in Northwich

Pushchairs	The paths in the parkland are flat and gravelled. The route along the lake is bumpy in parts, but easily manageable. Avoid the last section through Hopyards Wood and follow the pushchair route back to car park

1. Walk through the decorative wooden archway at the right of the car park. Follow the path, passing an information board on your left, then bear left along the wide driveway.

☺ Q: (AT THE ARCHWAY) This archway is a sculpture – a piece of art. There are many animals included in it – how many can you spot?

   A: There is a badger, a frog, a squirrel, a rabbit, a fox, a mouse, and several birds, including an woodpecker, a heron and an owl

2. At the junction continue straight ahead, passing the toilets and information on your right, signed for the site of the old Hall.

☺ The park was once the grounds of a large house and the low walls and steps show where the old hall once stood. The house was built over 150 years ago as a family home ... quite a big one! Later it was sold and became a club for rich country gentlemen. During the Second World War the house and grounds were used as a Prisoner of War camp, where foreign soldiers lived. Then in 1968 the house had to be demolished because it was in a bad state and needed too many repairs. So the hall lasted for 126 years, which isn't very long at all for a large country house. Some other halls in Cheshire are several hundreds of years old.

   Between the rows of trees was the main driveway to the hall, which horses and carriages, and later cars, would drive along.

3. Continue along the main path. After the site of the old Hall, the path enters an area of trees, with a high wall over on the left.

☺ The high wall over on the left once surrounded the kitchen garden of the old Hall, where all the vegetables and herbs were grown for use in the Hall. Today it is a garden centre.

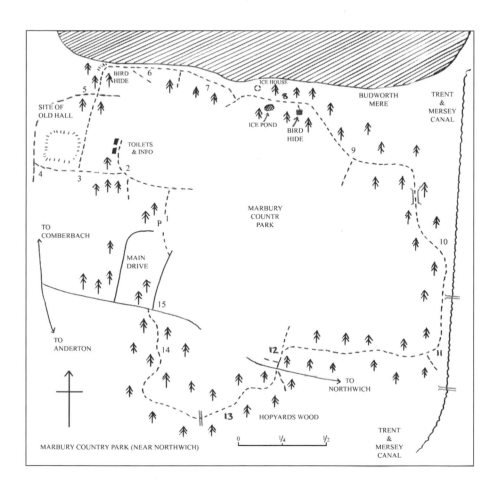

BIRD HIDE
SITE OF OLD HALL
ICE HOUSE
BUDWORTH MERE
TRENT & MERSEY CANAL
ICE POND
BIRD HIDE
TOILETS & INFO
MARBURY COUNTR PARK
TO COMBERBACH
P
MAIN DRIVE
TO ANDERTON
TO NORTHWICH
HOPYARDS WOOD
TRENT & MERSEY CANAL
MARBURY COUNTRY PARK (NEAR NORTHWICH)
0   1/4   1/2

4. **At the T-junction bear right, signed for Budworth Mere. The path winds slightly downhill to a wide tarmac avenue. Bear left down the set of steps to the bird hide.**

☺ (AT THE HIDE) This is called a "hide". It is a place where you can sit and watch the birds on the lake, without them being able to see you. If you look through the slits you should be able to see the lake and the reeds along the opposite banks. There are many different types of water bird that visit the lake, including mallards, herons, coots and swans. How many can you spot? There is a chart showing pictures of the birds, to help you tell which are which.

Someone who is interested in birds and birdwatching is called an "ornithologist". Perhaps you are an ornithologist?

5. **Continue along the path, going down the steps on the left to join the lakeside, passing behind the boathouse. (A short way ahead there is a ramp for use by pushchairs/wheelchairs.)**

☺ Over the lake you should be able to see a church tower in the village of Great Budworth, a few miles away. You may also see boats or windsurfers on the far side of the lake.

Along the edges of the water there may be a green floating weed, called "algae", which is eaten by fish and other animals. Close to the water, and in fact, growing in the water, there are several willow trees, which grow well in damp places, so they are often found close to rivers, lakes or swamps.

There is no swimming allowed in the lake. The lake is reserved for ducks and birds, and they wouldn't be too happy if there were people splashing about in the water! Also, there is a lot of weed growing under the water, which could wrap around a person's legs. Water is very dangerous, so never play near to it without an adult.

7. **At the junction keep left along the main wide gravel path, with the lake still visible through the trees on the left.**

Escape route: bear right and keep straight ahead for the car park.

8. **The path leads away from the lake – at the junction bear left, passing a small pond on your right.**

☺ Look out in the trees on the left for what looks like a round hole made of brick. This was once the entrance to an ice house, which was like a room underground where blocks of ice could be stored right through the year. The ice would have been used at the hall for keeping food cold and fresh, and in drinks, of course. It is colder underground and there would be no sunlight to warm it up, so even in hot, sunny weather the ice would not melt.

Over on the right of the path is the ice pond, where blocks of ice were cut in the winter and moved over to the ice house. Small chunks of ice would be taken to the hall when they were needed. It's a lot less trouble using a freezer, isn't it?

9. Avoid minor paths off in each direction, including a path on your right to a woodland bird hide. Follow the main path, which soon leads downhill to a wooden bridge crossing a drainage ditch. After the bridge continue along the path, moving away from the mere.

   Escape route: at the junction bear right signed for the car park. Take the second path on the right, between open fields, and continue to the car park.

☺ The ground here is soft and sandy, perfect for rabbits to burrow into. Can you find any rabbit holes? There are certainly many rabbits living in the woods. Perhaps if you are quiet and look carefully you will see one.

10. At the junction bear left, signed for Anderton Nature Park. Keep to the main path – it winds frequently, but is easy to follow. Keep to the main path which soon bears around to the right. Continue to the canal.

Marbury Country Park entrance

☺ This is the Trent and Mersey Canal, which was built in 1777 to transport goods from Stoke on Trent, where pottery was, and still is, made. Soon the Cheshire salt mines were also using the canal to carry their salt. The nearby town of Northwich is well known as a salt mining town.

11. **Bear right along the canal path. Avoid the footbridge over the canal.**

☺ Can you see any canal boats? They no longer carry salt or pottery, which will now go by rail, or most likely by road. The canals are used mainly for pleasure, for boating holidays.

12. **After a short way the path bears away from the canal and leads into the trees. At the junction continue ahead, signed for the car park. This path runs between a gravel track on the right and a concrete driveway over on the left.**

    Escape route/pushchair route: at the junction bear right, then take the first path on the left between open fields which will take you back to the car park/toilets etc.

13. **Carefully cross the driveway and enter the woods opposite, taking the right hand path as it leads slightly downhill.**

☺ There are many different trees in the woods, including sycamores. Can you recognise them? They are quite common in towns and can be found in parks or in peoples' gardens. In the autumn they have seeds in "keys" or "helicopters" which blow away with the wind. If it is autumn, you will probably see lots of them on the ground.

14. **Follow the steps leading downhill to the stream. Do not cross the bridge. Follow the path which runs alongside the stream for some way.**

☺ This stream is called Cogshall Brook and it has sandy banks, as the soil here, and in most of Cheshire, is very sandy. Along the brook there are nettles and blackberry bushes, and many trees with overhanging branches.
    The "keys" or "helicopters" contain the seeds of the sycamore tree.

All trees have seeds, which can grow into new trees. There are several elderberry trees in the woods. See if you can spot any. They have clusters of green berries in the summer, which ripen and turn purple or black in the autumn. The seeds are inside the berries. There are also oak trees in the woods. The seed of the oak tree is an acorn, which you have probably seen many times. See if you can find any acorns on the ground.

15. **The path eventually winds away from the stream, and there are two small footbridges over drainage ditches. Follow the path uphill, finally a set of steps lead up to the driveway.**

☺ There is a lot of ivy nearby, which covers large areas of the ground and grows up the trunks of trees. It has tiny suckers so that it can attach itself to the bark. Ivy is an "evergreen" plant, which means that it does not lose its leaves in the autumn, but stays green all the year round.

16. **Cross the driveway and take the trackway opposite. After a short way bear left through the barbecue and picnic area and continue to the car park.**

Marbury Country Park Checklist

☐ A BLACK AND WHITE COW	☐ A CANAL BOAT
☐ A SWAN	☐ A CHURCH TOWER
☐ A PERSON WITH A DOG	☐ A WOODEN STATUE
☐ A DUCK	☐ A SQUIRREL
☐ A HOLLY BUSH	☐ A WHITE CAR
☐ A WOODEN FOOTBRIDGE	☐ A HORSE

17. Middlewood Way and Macclesfield Canal

An ideal training walk for children along the Middlewood Way – a disused railway converted into a footpath/cycleway/bridleway, which runs from Marple to Macclesfield, providing miles of pleasant and varied walking – and it's completely flat!

Starting point	Nelson Pit car park (SJ946833), off Lyme Road, Higher Poynton
By rail	Middlewood Station (SJ946848) on the Manchester to Buxton line. From the steps from the "trains to Manchester" platform bear left along the Middlewood way and continue from Direction 7
By bus	Buses from Stockport to Higher Poynton. Get off by the Boar's Head pub – cross over the road, over the railway bridge to Nelson Pit car park. Start from Direction 1
Distance	2½ miles
Terrain	Good level paths for most of the way
Maps	OS Landrangers 109
Public Toilets	Toilets at Nelson Pit car park
Refreshments	A pub near Nelson Pit, café on the canal
Pushchairs	Good, level paths along the canal, though the woodland stretch afterwards is impassable for pushchairs and it would be advisable to return the same way

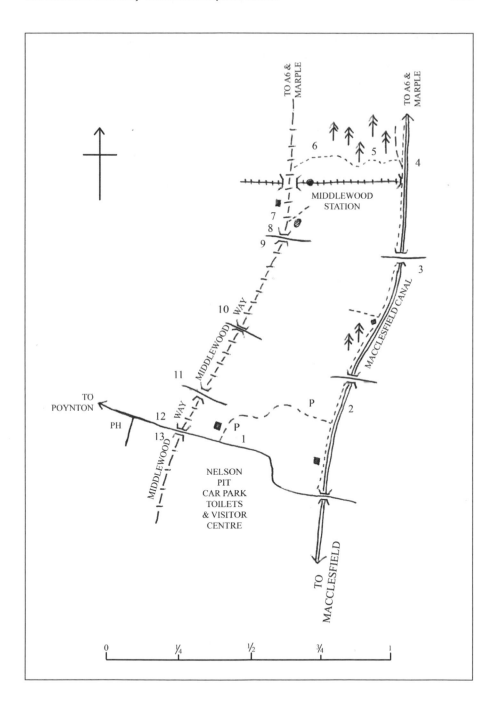

1. **Starting in the lower part of the Nelson Pit car park, pass the
    visitor centre/toilets on your left and continue along the
    pathway leading to the upper car park. At the top cut straight
    across the car park and go through the gate onto the canal
    towpath. Bear left.**

    *Just to the right, on the canal side is a small shop/café with
    seats outside.*

☺ This is the Macclesfield Canal. Canals are manmade, unlike rivers, which
   are natural. They were built so that boats could carry food, cotton and
   coal from town to town. Canals can be quite deep, so don't go near the
   edge. If you can't already swim you might like to think about having
   swimming lessons.
     There will probably be boats along the canal. The canal boats are
   long and narrow, and are called narrowboats. They are often used for
   boating holidays, but some people actually live on them. The boats are
   often decorated in bright colours and might have flowers or hanging
   baskets on them.

2. **Continue along the towpath, passing under bridge 14.**

☺ There will probably be ducks on the water. Mallards are the most
   common type of duck. The males have green heads; the females are
   brown. You may also see white geese, Canada geese (which have black
   necks) and swans.
     Over on the right, across the open countryside keep a look out for
   Lyme Cage – the square tower on the top of the hill. This was once a
   summerhouse for the people who lived at nearby Lyme Hall. You may
   also see herds of deer in the fields, which also belong to Lyme.

   *Escape route: to cut the walk very short look out for the footpath
   on the left after the woodland. Follow the track for approx ¼ mile,
   then bear left down the steps before the bridge; bear left along
   the Middlewood Way; for Middlewood Station bear right; for
   Nelson Pit car park bear left and continue from Direction 10.*

☺ There were once many coal mines in the area, and the canals were used
   to carry coal to the markets to be sold. The last coal mine in this area
   closed in the 1930s. When the railways were built the canals were used

less and less for carrying goods, because the railways were much quicker.

3. **Pass under bridge 13 and continue ahead. The towpath joins a trackway. Keep ahead with the canal.**

☺ There should be trees on your left now and hawthorn hedges, which are prickly and have red berries in the winter, providing food for hungry birds. Keep a look out far below for the railway line which passes in a tunnel under the canal.

4. **Where the trackway splits keep left – almost immediately look out for the signed footpath leading through the woodland away from the canal. This is signed as the Ladybrook Valley.**

☺ Q: There are many silver birch trees in the woods; they have slim trunks with peeling white bark. What is a young tree called?
  A: A sapling

5. **There are frequent yellow arrows to point the way, but the path splits regularly and winds around muddy areas. Keep as straight ahead as possible, running parallel with the railway which should be over on your left.**

☺ There are many different plants in the woods, including nettles, brambles and a tall plant called Himalayan balsam, which has pink flowers in the summer; in the autumn it has pods which pop open if you touch them, spraying the seeds of the plant around. They can often be found growing in damp areas. See if you can see any.

6. **Various other paths lead off, but keep straight ahead. The path crosses the edge of a grassy meadow. (Keep the trees on your left.) At the far side go through the gap in the wooden fence and join the trackway. Keep left and follow the path as it leads downhill to the Middlewood Way. Bear left and cross the bridge over the railway.**

☺ This railway line goes between Manchester and Buxton. The engines that pull the carriages are either diesel or electric. Steam trains haven't run on these lines for many years.

7. Continue ahead along the Middlewood Way.

Be aware of others using the path, especially horses and cyclists. One side of the track is for pedestrians, the other for walkers – cyclists seem to use both sides.

☺ At this point there is quite a drop over on the right. This was once a railway, and railways have to be fairly flat, so in places like this a bank would have to be built for the rails to be laid on. This bank is called an embankment.

Q: Look out for the house on the right. How many chimneys does it have?

A: Two – with many chimney pots

7. Avoid the path to the left, keep straight ahead.

☺ Look out for the small pond on your left, with reeds and bulrushes around its edges. Can you see any animals or insects around the pond? Look out for frogspawn in the spring – this is a clear "jelly" which contains the eggs of frogs. The eggs hatch into tadpoles, which grow tails and become frogs. In the summer look out for dragonflies, which hover above the water. They are long flying insects, usually a bright blue colour.

8. Pass under the bridge and continue straight ahead, keeping to the lower path. (The footpath at this point is on the left, bridleway on the right.)

☺ Q: Look for the wooden sign under the bridge. How far is Marple from here?

A: 4.6 kilometres

The line is now running through what is called a cutting. Because the railways have to be flat sometimes a "cutting" has to be made through the land, so there are banks on either side of you. These banks are now covered with plants and trees and attract many birds, animals and insects. Look out for rabbits, squirrels and foxes.

9. Pass under the bridge, continue ahead.

☺ Q: Here is another bridge. How far is Marple now?
    A: 5 kilometres

In the summer there are many plants growing along the sides of the pathway, including clover with purple flowers, nettles, brambles and rosebay willow herb, which is a tall plant with clusters of pink flowers at the top; it can often be found in hedgerows or growing on waste ground.

10. **Pass under Barlow House bridge and continue ahead along the trackway – avoiding the steps to the left.**

☺ Q: Of the plants growing alongside the trackway, which could sting you?
    A: A nettle

    Q: And which has prickles?
    A: A bramble, or blackberry bush

11. **When the path splits keep right, passing under Lyme Road bridge to the picnic site.**

☺ Here is yet another bridge. This one has a brick support in the middle because it carries a road across it and needs to support all the heavy modern traffic.
    This was once a station for the railway. Can you see the old platform on the right, where people would board their trains?

12. **Take the ramp on the left just after Lyme Road bridge. Keep left, up the steps and cross over back to Nelson Pit car park.**

Rail users – to return to the station skip to Direction 1.

Middlewood Way Checklist

☐	A CANAL BOAT	☐	A DUCK
☐	A SWAN	☐	A RABBIT
☐	A SQUIRREL	☐	A COW
☐	A HORSE	☐	A PINK FLOWER
☐	A BRIDGE	☐	A NETTLE
☐	A PICNIC TABLE	☐	A DOG

18. Over Peover

Not to be confused with its sister village, Lower Peover, which is a few miles to the west. Over Peover, also known as Peover Superior, is a flat and attractive rural area overlooked by the Jodrell Bank Telescope, and as a bonus it has a selection of fine inns on its doorstep. Peover, incidentally, is pronounced "peever" and is anglo-saxon, meaning "bright river" after the small river, the Peover Eye, that runs close by.

Starting point	Stocks Lane, Over Peover (SJ780741), close to the sharp bend in the road, where there is an old signpost pointing to, amongst other places, Peover Hall. Room for careful parking along the sides of Stocks Lane Over Peover can be reached from the A50 Knutsford to Holmes Chapel road. Turn off at the Whipping Stocks Inn, signed for Radbroke Hall and Stocks Lane. One mile along the lane there is space for parking, just before the road bears round to the left
By bus	Services to Over Peover from Macclesfield, Knutsford and Northwich
Distance	Entire route - 6 miles Shorter route - 4 miles Plus various escape routes
Terrain	Flat footpaths or trackways for most of the way. The woodland along the Peover Eye stretch will probably be quite muddy in wet weather and can easily be avoided using escape route
Maps	OS Landrangers 118
Public Toilets	Toilets at the Whipping Stocks Inn for patrons only. No public toilets

Refreshments	Whipping Stocks, Stocks Lane
Pushchairs	Unsuitable for pushchairs

1. **From the sharp bend in the road, follow the narrow driveway signed as a footpath to Peover Hall, passing a row of small brick cottages on the left. (Also signed for the Village Hall.)**

☺ You should pass a cottage which was, until recent years, the village Post Office. Can you guess which one? In case you can't, it was the one with the post box in the wall next to its front door. In the garden close to the door there is an old water pump, which was used to pump water up out of the ground before running water was fitted. It is no longer in use. Imagine having to go outside on a cold winter's day every time you wanted some water.

2. **Pass the long wooden building (which is the Village Hall) and continue along the drive, going through the white gates onto the Peover Hall Estate.**

☺ (AT THE HOUSE ON THE RIGHT) This is Peover Cottage. It is built of brick, and has a roof of stone slabs. Over the door there is a "coat of arms", which all rich and powerful families had. This coat of arms is quite worn and difficult to see, but it has a shield on it and two helmets from suits of armour.

3. **Continue along the drive, passing the stables on the right and avoid all turnings off the driveway. Instead keep straight ahead, through a gate along a fenced avenue of lime trees.**

☺ These rows of trees have been planted like this to form an attractive walkway which leads to Peover Hall. On either side there are fields and you may see sheep, cows or horses grazing in them. In the winter the horses may have coats on to keep them warm.

4. **At the end of the avenue climb the stile and cross the footbridge.**

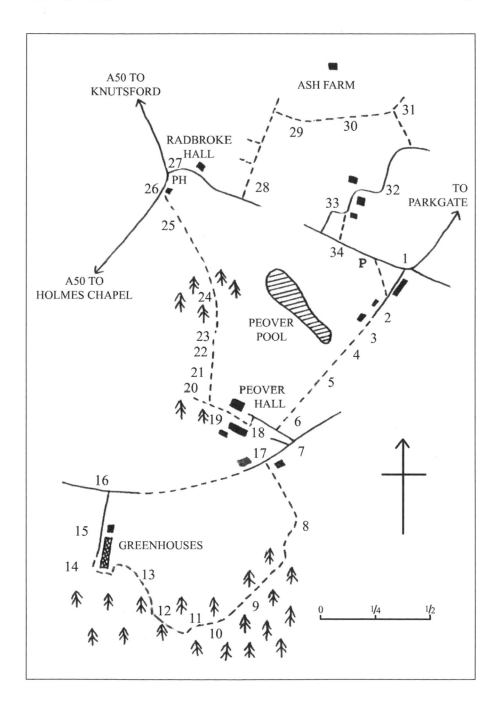

☺ This is Peover Pool – on both sides of the bridge. Along the edges of
the pool there are many reeds and thistles. In spring and summer, you
will see lilies floating on the surface of the water. The flowers close at
night and only become fully open by about midday, or not at all if the
weather is bad. In spring you might see "frogspawn" in the reeds
around the edge of the pond. Frogspawn is hundreds of frog eggs which
are kept safe in a sort of clear jelly. The female frog lays about 3000
eggs in March and it takes 2 or 3 weeks for them to hatch, depending
on how warm the weather is.

Q: Do you know what a baby frog is called?
A: It isn't really a frog at all. It is a tadpole. When it first hatches
      it has a tail, but no legs. As it grows bigger, legs begin to grow
      until it becomes a fully grown frog, and can live on land as well as
      in water.

5. Continue straight ahead across the parkland.

Peover Hall and Church

☺ Keep a look out (TO THE LEFT) for the huge dish of the Jodrell Bank Radio Telescope, which you should be able to see between the trees. The dish is directed up into the sky and can pick up movements in space. It has been used to track many of the rockets that have been launched from America and Russia.

Also look for Peover Hall, which should come into view between the trees. (AHEAD AND TO THE RIGHT) The hall was built by Sir Ralph Mainwaring in 1585, which means it is over 400 years old. His family lived there for many years, and the last Lady Mainwaring gave all her servants red knitted jackets for Christmas, so that they would stand out and she would be able to make sure they were hard at work. Today, the hall is owned by another family.

6. **Climb the stile at the opposite end of the field which will bring you onto the main drive of Peover Hall, close to the ornamental gates of the Hall; here turn left, heading away from the Hall, along the driveway which passes beneath overhanging trees.**

   Escape route: to avoid the woods in bad weather, or to make the route 2 miles shorter, skip to Direction 18.

7. **Continue ahead (avoiding the immediate turning leading back, signed for the church. Bear right along the main trackway, passing a farm driveway on the left. Just after the farm, take the stile on the left and continue towards the woods, keeping the wire fence on your left.**

☺ Q: There are often horses in these fields. Do you know what a female horse is called?
   A: A female horse is called a mare. A male is called a stallion

8. **At the bottom of the field bear right and follow the edge of the woods for a short way until you come across a gateway and footpath signpost pointing into the woods themselves. Follow the path downhill between the trees. Stick to the main path, which is easy to follow – it's the muddy one!**

☺ These are mixed woods. That means there are many different types of trees here, including oak, sycamore and horse chestnut, and there are many rhododendron bushes, which have dark green leaves all the year round. Through the summer months they have large, colourful flowers, often red, pink, white or lilac.

Q: What colour is lilac?
A: A sort of pale purple. Most wild rhododendrons are this colour

9. Follow the path downhill to the river and bear right. If the path becomes hard to follow at any point, look for white paint dots on the trees which indicate the way.

☺ This small river is called the Peover Eye. Notice how the bottom of the stream is covered in sand, because the stone beneath the ground is made of sand. Millions of years ago, long before there were people, much more of the planet was covered in water than it is today, and the Cheshire Plain was at the bottom of the sea, which is why there is so much sand in the county.

10. Do not cross at the footbridge over the river. Continue along the path which keeps fairly close to the river for some way. Remember to follow the white dots on the trees. The path crosses over various small bridges over tributary streams and boggy areas.

☺ These woods are very dark and mysterious, and very quiet. Unless it is the busiest time of the weekend you might not see anyone at all here, but there are eyes watching you ... look out for rabbits hiding in the undergrowth, keeping still, waiting until you pass before they move, and squirrels running along the branches above you, or disappearing up the trunks of the tall trees. There are many insects as well. Keep a look out for spiders hanging from webs in front of you, and try not to walk into them.

11. The path undulates for a while, but still keeps fairly close to the river.

☺ Conkers come from horse chestnut trees, but you will only find them in the autumn. Only pick them off the ground, never try to knock them from the trees, as this can damage the tree and also you may get in trouble if you are caught!

12. The path crosses a further two bridges, and then bears uphill, away from the river, through rhododendron bushes. Keep to the main path, passing a small pond on your right. Towards the top of the woods (with farmed fields visible ahead) the path bears to the right – with the fields visible occasionally on your right.

13. Follow the path down into a gully, cross the footbridge and continue uphill towards the greenhouses. Bear left, with the greenhouses on your right.

Four legged friends – horses at Peover Hall

☺ (AT THE GREENHOUSE) Glasshouses or greenhouses are used for growing plants that need warmth, that might otherwise die outside. What can you see growing inside? There might be young tomato plants, and almost certainly colourful flowers like chrysanthemums. If you ever buy flowers for somebody, it is most likely that they were grown in a greenhouse, like this. Sometimes you can see people inside cutting the flowers, so they can be put into bunches and sold.

14. Bear right at the end of the greenhouses, and right again, so you are now walking along the other side of the greenhouses.

15. Pass the farmhouse and continue along the lane, passing further greenhouses. At the junction bear right along the lane.

☺ Q: What is the name of the house that you pass on your right?
   A: Misty View

16. Continue ahead – in a short way the lane becomes a rough trackway and is surrounded by woodland. Follow this gently winding trackway for half a mile.

☺ Q: What are the names of the brick houses you will eventually pass
           on the left?
    A: Saint Anthony's

**17. Keep straight ahead after the Saint Anthony's houses, pass the
footpath on the right, then take the second left turning and
return along the driveway to the ornamental gates of Peover
Hall.**

*Escape route: climb the stile to the right of the ornamental gates
and retrace your steps across the parkland to the starting point –
keeping straight ahead.*

**18. Take the driveway to the left of the ornamental gates,
alongside the stable block. (Do not go through the gates to the
Hall.)**

☺ Q: This was once a stable block, where the horses lived. Lady
           Mainwaring of Peover Hall had it built for her son, Thomas.
           But in which year?
    A: 1654. There is a plaque over the door with an inscription and date

Next to the stables is a building which looks quite similar. This is the
Coach House, where carriages would be kept. It was built over 100
years after the stables. On the front of the building there is a clock
and on the roof there is a small belltower.

    Q: Close by there is a set of steps which don't lead anywhere. Can
           you guess what they were for?
    A: Ladies would go up the steps to help them climb onto a horse

**19. After the Coach House turn left through the white gates, then
bear right alongside the brick garden wall.**

*The gate into the gardens is on the right. The gardens are open to
the public on Monday and Thursday afternoons. Payment is by an
honesty box.*

☺ Look out on the right for a strange piece of square stone with lines and
   numbers on it. Do you know what it is? It is a sundial. It can be used to

tell the time, but only when the sun shines. The metal bar casts a shadow on the numbers, so it is like the hand of a clock. See if you can tell the time by it.

Towards the end of the drive you might notice several small gravestones. This is the pets' graveyard, where the owners of the Hall buried their animal companions.

20. **Take the paved pathway to the right, directly before the sundial, passing through the trees to the Church of Saint Lawrence.**

☺ The oldest parts of the church are 550 years old, but most of it was rebuilt nearly 200 years ago. In the graveyard, close to the bench, there is a large yew tree. Yews have dark green, needle-like leaves, which they do not lose in the winter. Yews can live for thousands of years.

21. **From the church, go along the tree-lined walk which runs past the graveyard. This rejoins the gravel pathway through the gardens, bear right along this.**

☺ There is a tall wall on the left. On the other side is the Kitchen Garden, where all the fruit and vegetables were grown for the Lord of the Manor and his family. The huts along the wall will have been for the gardeners, where they kept their tools, and probably had five minutes rest, safely out of sight of Lady Mainwaring.

22. **Continue ahead, avoiding all gateways and paths into the gardens on either side, which are private. Pass by the steps on the left and keep to the main path. Continue through the trees and go through the wooden gate. Bear left to a stile, then right to a further stile; cross this and keep right along the edge of the field.**

☺ The long brick wall (ON THE RIGHT) separates the gardens of the hall from the parkland. You might be able to see a gold ball above the wall, which is part of the roof of a summerhouse, where the Lord of the Manor could sit with his family on warm summer days.

During the Second World War the hall was used as a headquarters for the American Army. Hundreds of soldiers lived in huts in the grounds around you.

23. Keep to the edge of the field and take the stile in the fence at the end. Continue through the small wooded area to a further stile; after this continue straight ahead through a grassy field and cross a stile in the fence on the right. Bear left along the stony driveway.

☺ There are good views back over the parkland to the hall and church, rising out of the trees.

    You will soon come to a pond. In fact, it is the other end of Peover Pool, which you passed earlier. Again there are reeds and rushes along its banks, and weed on the surface of the water. Perhaps there are some ducks or coots.

24. Cross the bridge and continue along the driveway.

☺ Look out for another pond (ON THE RIGHT TOWARDS THE END OF THE NEXT STAND OF TREES). It is only small and is covered by floating "blanket weed" which tiny creatures, like water beetles and snails, can eat. The more plants there are in and around a pond, the more wild creatures will live there, as the plants provide food, shelter and protection. Even in the winter there is plenty of life under the water. A small pond like this will easily freeze over, and the layer of ice, rather than making the water cold, stops any more cold from getting in, so it keeps the temperature up a bit. In the autumn dead leaves will fall from the trees into the pond and will eventually sink to the bottom, making warm layers for the underwater creatures to live in throughout the winter.

    Soon after the pond there are more horse chestnut trees forming an "avenue" along the driveway. They have wooden fences around them to protect them from cows and other animals.

25. Continue through the white gates, passing the entrance lodge on the right.

☺ This is Knutsford Lodge, which was built nearly 200 years ago. If you look carefully you'll notice that tree trunks were used to make the corners of the house. It has unusual arched windows, and many colourful hanging baskets of flowers. In pots there are small monkey puzzle trees, which have dark, prickly leaves. They are supposed to get their name because monkeys cannot puzzle out how to climb them.

26. Bear right to the Whipping Stocks pub.

The Whipping Stocks has a beer garden and children are welcome.

☺ The hanging sign outside the inn shows a set of "stocks" after which the inn, and the road it is built on, are named. As you can see on the picture, the man is locked in the "stocks" as a form of punishment, because he has obviously committed a crime. The villagers would often throw tomatoes and rotten vegetables at people in the stocks, or they sometimes got whipped. You wouldn't want to break the law again after a punishment like that.

27. Take great care crossing the road in front of the whipping stocks, then follow the path (behind the hedge at this point) to the right along Stocks Lane. Pass Radbroke Hall (Barclays Bank) on the left, crossing over both of its driveways, then take the public footpath on the left, running along the edge of a field.

Escape route: to return to the starting point continue along the lane for just over half a mile.

28. Keep straight ahead, through an open gateway into the next field. Avoid the two stiles off to the left, but at the second one bear right across the field, to the left of the hedge.

☺ The hedge is made up mainly of hawthorns. As you might guess from the name, they have sharp thorns. In autumn they have bright red berries, which are called "haws", which makes up the first part of their name, Haw-thorn. The berries attract many small birds which feed on them through the cold winter months when there is little else to eat.

29. At the end of the field go through the gap in the hedge bear right for a short way to the small pond. Here bear left, crossing the open field. go through a gap in the hedge and continue ahead, now with a hedge on your right.

30. Keep ahead at the junction. The path soon becomes a bridleway enclosed between hedges. Keep with the main path;

after some way this bears around to the right; avoid the stile to the left. Continue ahead.

☺ This trackway is used by farmers. Perhaps you can see the marks of a tractor on the ground, or horses' hoofprints. Again, the hedges are mainly hawthorns, but there are also other plants, such as nettles and ivy and tall pink flowers called rosebay willow herb. The hedges provide shelter and homes for many wild animals like field mice and rabbits, as well as small birds like sparrows and robins.

31. At the end of the track bear right along the lane. There is an open field on the right and woodland on the left which is sometimes used as a caravan site. After the woods there are wide open fields on both sides. Take the track to the left. The track to the right leads only to a farmhouse.

☺ The crops change in the fields from year to year. Wheat and potatoes are often grown in Cheshire and so is sweetcorn and sometimes greens, such as cabbage or sprouts. The fields are often left as grass, to feed cows and sheep. If there is a crop in the field, see if you can tell what it is.

32. The track crosses over a stream, and soon after bears right around to the right. Avoid the signed footpath on the corner and continue towards newhall farm. Keep straight ahead, go through the gate and again continue ahead. Bear left after the brick barn.

☺ Q: The brick barn on your left is very old. Can you find a date when it was bilt?
   A: 1711. The date can be seen over a door towards the back of the building. Notice that many doors and windows in the barn have been bricked up over the years. You can tell where they were because the bricks used are a slightly different colour.

33. Continue along the drive and go through the five bar gate straight ahead; cross the large field, aiming directly for the brick house on the road. Cross the stile in the hedge in front of the house.

☺ Q: What is the date on the brick house opposite the stile?
  A: 1937

34. Bear left along the lane, which will return you to the starting
    point at the crossroads.

Over Peover Checklist

☐ A HORSE	☐ A COW
☐ A HORSECHESTNUT TREE	☐ A DUCK OR COOT
☐ A "SATELLITE DISH"	☐ A TRACTOR
☐ A GREENHOUSE	☐ A CHURCH
☐ A RABBIT	☐ A WHITE FARMHOUSE
☐ A WATER PUMP	☐ A GOLD CLOCK

19. Overton Hill

The first part of the walk offers views over the Mersey estuary, Frodsham, Ellesmere Port and towards Liverpool. It is certainly a very interesting sight; the second part of the walk is a total contrast, through very attractive woodlands, along the early stages of the long distance footpath, The Sandstone Trail.

Starting point	Beacon Hill Sandstone Trail car park (SJ519766). From Frodsham take the B5152 Delamere Road. After three quarters of a mile bear right along Manley Road, signed "Mersey View 1 mile". After half a mile bear right along Simons Lane, signed for the golf course. The car park is further along, well signed, on the right
By rail	The nearest station is at Frodsham, a mile away. It is an uphill climb through houses
Distance	3 miles
Terrain	Footpaths and short distances along quiet lanes. Some easy climbing over stepped sandstone, which can be avoided by using the second escape route Note: all escape routes use footpaths crossing the vast golf course. If you consider this unsafe, then stick to the entire route
Maps	OS Landrangers 117
Public Toilets	None
Refreshments	Nowhere in the vicinity
Pushchairs	Not suitable at all

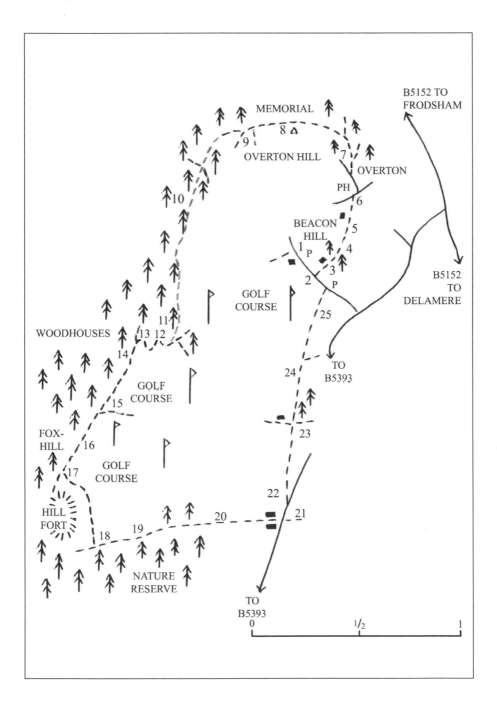

1. **From main car park bear left along the lane, downhill.**

☺ Notice the radio mast near the car park – you should be able to see
this many times throughout the walk. It will let you know how far from
the car park you are.

2. **After a short way look out for the footpath on the left
    alongside a driveway. Follow this as it leads slightly uphill.**

☺ Q: The gate next to the footpath has the name of a house on it.
        What is the name?
   A: Overhill Cottage

3. **When the drive bears left to the house keep straight ahead
    along the grassy path.**

☺ Notice the old lamp post on the right. The path now passes between
many thick bushes, most of which are prickly, including holly and
hawthorn, and watch out for the nettles!

4. **Go through the five bar gate. Cross the hotel driveway and
    continue straight ahead, with a wooden fence now on the
    right. The path leads downhill around the hotel gardens.**

☺ There are views on the right over the houses of Frodsham, and on the
left are the grounds of a hotel, with many trees and rhododendron bushes.

5. **Follow the main path, which is fairly well-trodden. After the
    woods pass in front of the bungalow and continue to the road.
    Bear right, downhill.**

☺ Q: What is the name of the pub on the left?
   A: The Belle Monte Hotel

The Belle Monte has a beer garden and family room.

6. **Bear left, passing the front of the pub. Look out on the right
    directly after the car park for a narrow path leading downhill
    between bushes and trees. Follow this, bearing left almost
    immediately. Keep to the upper path at all times.**

☺ These are mixed woods with many oak trees and holly bushes. Some of the tree trunks have ivy growing on them, and it also grows over the ground in places. There are also blackberry bushes with their long, prickly stems, and bilberries; short bushes with light green leaves and black/purple berries in the autumn.

7. **At the fork keep left along the upper path, signed for Delamere and Beeston. (There should be frequent signs as this is part of the long distance Sandstone Trail.) After some way bear left up the steps and continue to the stone monument.**

Take care of unfenced cliffs at all times!

☺ (AT THE MONUMENT) This monument is built of sandstone blocks, and is a memorial to the men from Frodsham (below) who died in the First and Second World Wars. From here there are views over the River Mersey as it makes its way towards the sea. If you look to the right you should be able to make out where the River Weaver joins the Mersey. Also, you may be able to see the Manchester Ship Canal, which runs below between the Mersey and the motorway.

Overton War Memorial

Close to the monument is a diagram showing all the things that can be seen from here, like the cathedral in Liverpool. It also tells you how far away things are.

Q: Snowdon is the highest mountain in England and Wales. How far away is it from here?
A: 58.5 miles

Q: Chester is the capital city of Cheshire. How far away is it from here?
A: 9.5 miles

8. **From the monument continue along the clifftop path, with the cliff on your right, passing the hotel on your far left. (Take**

care of the cliff edge.) Follow the path between the bushes and brambles. Keep to the upper path.

☺ After a short way there should be lots of colourful trees below you, and there are now fields and marshes between the motorway and the river.

9. Where the path splits follow the lower path, signed as part of the Sandstone Trail, leading slightly downhill through the woods. Avoid steps to either side, continue with the main path.

☺ The trees here are mainly oaks, from which acorns come. Keep a look out for squirrels, who like to eat acorns and can often be seen running along the branches and tree trunks. There are also many prickly holly bushes.

You should be able to see red sandstone cliffs to your left. As its name suggests, sandstone is made up of thousands of grains of sand.

Woodland path

10. After some way the path becomes rougher, sand and rock. Avoid the left turning into the "quarry" – continue ahead. You should soon be able to see a golf course over on your left. Continue ahead, the path now becomes narrower.

☺ You should pass a bench, where there is a view over to a hilltop partly covered with trees; this is Helsby Hill. From some angles many people think it looks like an old man's face. Can you see a face?

11. Continue to the signpost at a junction of paths. Follow the path to the right, signed for Delamere Forest, going down a set of steps.

Escape route: to return to the car park bear left at the signpost, signed for Beacon Hill car park. Follow the occasional posts across the golf course to an uphill path, which will bring you to a lane. Bear right, and the car park is just ahead on the left.

12. Keep to the upper path. Go down a further set of steps called "Baker's Dozen".

☺ Q: These steps are called "Baker's Dozen". How many are in a dozen? And how many steps are there?

   A: A dozen is twelve, but in the "olden days" if you went into a baker's and asked for a dozen bread rolls he would have given you twelve plus an extra one, making thirteen. (It probably wouldn't work today, but you could try it!)

☺ This path is part of a long distance path called the "Sandstone Trail". On the left you should be able to see a "cliff" of sandstone rock, with trees growing on the top and hanging over. Can you see their roots clinging to the rock?
   In the autumn, when the leaves fall, they gather in piles on the ground. Hedgehogs like to curl up among the warm, dry leaves beneath hedges or bushes. If you have a bonfire on November 5th, before lighting it you should check that no hedgehogs have crawled under the sticks and leaves, as a lot of them get killed this way. Hedgehogs are well known for their prickly backs. If they are frightened, they can roll into a ball and be safe from wild animals or dogs.

Have you noticed that in the spring there don't seem to be leaves on the ground, so what happens to all the leaves that fall in the autumn? They rot and break down, turning eventually into soil, which will feed other plants and trees. In nature, nothing is wasted.

13. **Continue down the further sets of steps. At the bottom the path bears to the right. Continue to the sign post.**

☺ (AT THE SIGNPOST) The worn sandstone rock on the right is called "Jacob's Ladder" because it is like a stone staircase, and many people climb up it. Can you see the footholes that have worn in the stone? Sandstone is very soft and easily wears away. This type of wearing away is called "erosion" and can be quite a problem, as lots of human feet can badly damage footpaths and work has to be done to repair them. This kind of repair work to the countryside is called "conservation" and people who do it and care for the countryside are called "conservationists". Do you believe in conservation?

14. **From the signpost bear left signed Sandstone Trail/Delamere. The path heads slightly uphill, with the rockface visible on the left.**

☺ If you look over to the left of the path you should be able to see a small cave high up in the "cliff". Can you make out the footholes where people have climbed up to it? Don't try this; it's very dangerous.

15. **Cross the wooden "bridge" and continue up the path, cobbled in places. Avoid the stile on the left and continue ahead to the rocky outcrop, signed for the Sandstone Trail. The path now ascends the outcrop by a series of worn "steps". It is not difficult, but take care of the drop on the right.**

Escape route: to cut the route short, or to avoid the rocky climb, bear left over the stile and make your way through the bushes to a further stile. Keep straight ahead across the golf course, at first there is a hedge on the left. Continue to the sign post, then bear right. Keep straight ahead to a stile near the corner of the field. Follow the edge of the field towards the farm buildings. Continue straight through the farmyard, passing the farmhouse on the left (with a waterpump outside the door) and

*continue along the drive to the footpath on the left. Continue
from Direction 24.*

16. **At the top of the rocky outcrop continue along the main path.
The golf course should be visible on the left. Avoid the many
minor paths leading off into the trees. Make sure that the golf
course is in sight at all times.**

☺ The trees here are still mainly oaks, but there are also some holly
bushes, with their dark green, prickly leaves. There is also bracken,
which is the tall, fern-like plant that turns dry and brown in the winter.
   If you look over at the golf course you should be able to see what
look like large holes filled with sand. These are called "bunkers" and
the golfers have to avoid them. If their ball lands in a bunker it is
difficult to get it out again without cheating. The coloured flags mark
the holes that the golfers have to aim for.

17. **Bear left with the fence, now briefly leaving the Sandstone
Trail. The path leads slightly uphill through trees and
undergrowth. Do not stray onto the golf course. The path soon
bears to the right, leading steeply uphill.**

☺ The land rising on the right was once part of a hillfort, though nothing
can now be seen except these steep banks which would probably have
protected small wooden huts which people would have lived in
thousands of years ago.
   There are still many oak trees in this part of the woods, but there
are also birch trees. They have white trunks and diamond-shaped
leaves. Keep a look-out for toadstools which can often be found
growing under birches. If you see any look, but do not touch them , as
many toadstools and mushrooms are poisonous.

18. **Where the path splits keep left, with the fence to your left.
After some way the path rejoins the main Sandstone Trail.
Bear left along this and again keep the fence in sight on the
left.**

☺ The trees are almost all birches now, and there is a lot more of the
fern-like bracken growing beneath them. Look up at the branches of
the trees. Perhaps you can see a bird's nest. In the autumn or winter

when the leaves have fallen they are easy to spot. In the spring, birds build new nests and then the female lays eggs. One bird, usually the mother, will sit on the eggs at all times to keep them warm. When the chicks hatch the parent birds will bring them food to the nest until they are able to look after themselves.

Some birds, like the black and white magpie, eat other birds' eggs, and sometimes even small chicks, and so will squirrels if there aren't enough nuts and berries for them.

Magpies, once they find a mate, usually stay together for life, so if you see a magpie take a look around, there will probably be another somewhere close by. Magpies have a habit of stealing bright, shiny objects, like silver or jewellery, and taking it back to their nests.

19. The path bears to the left, around the field edge, soon after which there is a signpost. Keep straight ahead and follow the path uphill via the wide steps. Continue ahead.

☺ Amongst the birch trees there are a few rowan trees. These have orange-red berries in the autumn and winter. Can you spot any?

Horses in winter coats, near Overton Hill

20. The path becomes enclosed between a fence and hedge, crossing between farmed fields. Go through the five bar gate blocking the way ahead and continue along the track towards the houses.

☺ Q: On the right is a pair of semi-detached houses; that means they are joined together. How many chimneys are there on the roof?

A: Three

21. Continue along the track to the road. Bear left. (There are well-trodden grass verges along both sides.)

☺ Q: On the left, almost hidden in the bushes is the name of a house on a sign. If you can see the sign, what is the name of the house?

A: Shepherd's Cottage

22. After a short way go through the metal kissing gate on the left and follow the signed footpath, diagonally right, towards the transmitters on the hill.

☺ Down on the left are the woods you have just walked through. In the autumn they are very colourful, and a popular place for walkers, like yourself. In case you're getting tired, there isn't far to go now.

23. Go through another metal kissing gate. Cross the farm driveway and take the path opposite.

24. Follow the footpath, avoiding the stile to the right.

☺ Q: Over the wire mesh fence on the right there are often sheep grazing. Everyone knows that a baby sheep is called a lamb, but do you know what a male and female sheep are called?

A: The female is called a "ewe" and the male is called a "ram".

On the left there are views over the River Mersey, which is very wide here, on the last part of its journey to the sea. On the other side of the water is Liverpool. You should also be able to see the golf course.

25. The path opens onto the edge of the golf course. Continue straight ahead with the hedge on your left.

26. Bear left onto the lane, leading uphill. The walkers car park is
    in quarter of a mile on the right.

Overton Hill Checklist

☐ A COLOURED FLAG   ☐ A SQUIRREL

☐ A PERSON WITH A RUCKSACK   ☐ A BLACK AND WHITE COW

☐ A RABBIT HOLE   ☐ AN ACORN

☐ A MUSHROOM OR TOADSTOOL   ☐ A HORSE

☐ SOMEONE IN CHEQUERED   ☐ A TREE WITH RED BERRIES
   TROUSERS PLAYING GOLF   IN AUTUMN OR WHITE
                                        BLOSSOM IN SPRING

20. Peckforton

This has to be one of the finest walks in all Cheshire. A peaceful stroll through the gentle Peckforton Hills, beneath the shadow of two of Cheshire's most impressive monuments, the castles of Beeston and Peckforton – one the genuine article and one a well-constructed sham, but no less impressive. Sit outside at the Pheasant Inn overlooking the Cheshire Plain, make your own candle (if you're under 14!) at the Cheshire Workshops, see the haunted bridge, the stone elephant and idyllic village scenes. A memorable and varied day out.

Starting point	Sandstone Trail car park off Barracks Lane, next to the candle workshops, Higher Burwardsley
Distance	4 miles
Terrain	Good paths and trackways, some gentle climbing through the Peckforton Hills, lane-side verges
Maps	OS Landranger 117
Public Toilets	No public toilets at all. Facilities at Pheasant Inn, Cheshire Workshops for patrons only
Refreshments	Pheasant Inn, Higher Burwardsley Cheshire Workshops, Higher Burwardsley; restaurant/tea-room
Pushchairs	With some effort the route is navigable for pushchairs, though the return from Peckforton village is along a lane; it does have wide grass verges for much of the way, but not along its entirety. The escape routes are not suitable for pushchairs

Beyond the Sandstone Trail car park are the Candle Workshops, open daily from 10 to 5 and admission is free. Craftspersons can be watched at work making candles, glassblowing etc. Children from 5 to 14 can make their own candles. Also cafe, restaurant and toilets.

1. **From the car park bear left along the lane, then take the right turning almost immediately.**

☺ Q: Look at the side of the building on your left – there should be a plaque high up on the wall. There is a date on it, what is it?
   A: 1998

2. **At the crossroads go straight over, along Rock Lane. The lane winds slightly uphill between high hedges and overhanging trees. At the fork bear right, still uphill.**

☺ Q: What is the name of the farm on the left?
   A: Rockhouse Farm. It is built mainly of sandstone. In a short way the lane is cut into sandstone and you can clearly see the rock. It is usually a sandy red colour, like the farmhouse, but here it is covered with moss and lichen

3. **Keep straight ahead, passing a whitewashed cottage on the right bearing a plaque saying "Elephant Track". Continue along the trackway, signed for Bulkeley Hill.**

☺ This is called the Elephant Track, not because elephants walk along here, but because at one time there were cottages at the other end of the track and outside one of them was a life-size stone elephant. But more about that later...

4. **Keep ahead. The road degenerates into a stony trackway, signed for Stonehouse Lane. The path is level and passes between ferns and hedges, before woods begin on either side.**

☺ You may pass a field with horses in along the trackway. Also there may be Highland Cattle grazing. They have long horns and woolly coats. They originally came from Scotland, which is how they get their name.

5. **Avoid the footpath to the left and continue ahead.**

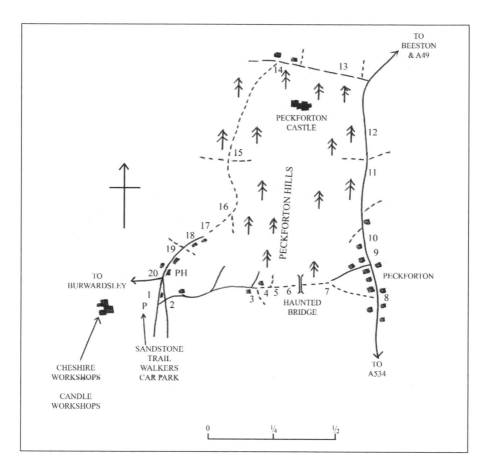

☺ You should pass another plantation of conifers. Can you recognise them? Some of the trees are much shorter than others, and were obviously planted later.

    Again, you may see rabbits and keep a look out for pheasants, a colourful bird with long tail feathers; there are many in these woods.

6. The path soon begins to descend. Keep straight ahead avoiding all other trackways and footpaths. Go under the sandstone bridge and continue ahead.

☺ (AT THE BRIDGE) This is called the Haunted Bridge and was once the main driveway of Peckforton Castle, which is now hidden in the trees.

Peckforton Castle Gatehouse

Horses and carriages would drive along here from the gatehouse to the castle entrance. It is supposed to be haunted by a servant woman who worked at the castle.

A morbid note for adults: she is supposed to carry a severed head beneath her arm. Try not to bump into her.

Pushchairs continue down the trackway and bear left at the bottom. Continue from Direction 9.

7. **Take the stile to the right immediately after the haunted bridge, heading straight across the field towards a fringe of trees, with cottages and farmhouses visible beyond. There are various stiles all quite close together, and the path is easy to follow, leading at last through an area of conifers. Bear left along the stony driveway to the lane.**

☺ This is the village of Peckforton. Most of the houses are very old, but some older than others. On the left is a thatched cottage with black and white walls. Notice how most of the other cottages look very much alike, with the same square chimneys, the same windows, painted the same colours. Lord Tollemache, who lived in the castle, owned all these houses and spent a fortune improving them for the villagers, which is when the diamond shaped windows were put in.

8. Bear left along the pavement.

☺ Now keep your eyes open for the elephant. (CLEARLY VISIBLE FROM THE PAVEMENT, IN A GARDEN ON THE LEFT.) It is carved from stone and is carrying a castle on its back. It was made by a stonemason who was working on Peckforton Castle, when it was being built. It stood outside his cottage near the Haunted Bridge, and when the cottage was pulled down it was moved here. It is thought the castle part was intended as a beehive, though it was probably never used as one. Why an elephant carrying a castle, you may be wondering? The only possible answer is that the family who owned the surrounding area several hundred years ago had an elephant and a castle on their "coat of arms" or Family Emblem.

9. Continue along the lane.

☺ After the stone elephant there is a small orchard (ALSO ON THE LEFT) with several apples and pear trees.

10. The pavement ends at the next cottage, but for most of the way there are grass verges along the lane on one side or the other.

☺ On the right you may notice several more apple trees, and in the hedgerows there are other fruits growing, such as blackberries and elderberries.

Q: You should be able to see the tall brick chimneys of the next cottage from some distance away. How many does it have?
A: Four, all in a row in the middle of the roof

Look out for Castle Cottage on the right, which has a water pump in its garden, which at one time would have been used to pump water

up out of the ground. When this was in use there were no taps and
no hot water! A tin bath in front of the fire was the best that was
available.

**11. Continue along the lane to the gatehouse of Peckforton
Castle.**

☺ This is the entrance to the grounds of Peckforton Castle – it is now a
posh hotel and restaurant. A gatekeeper would have lived in the house
to the right of the archway, to open the gates and allow visitors in.
High up in the trees is the castle itself – not visible from here, but you
might have seen it as you drove here. It was built 150 years ago as a
"stately home" but was made to look much older.

   This spot was chosen so that the castle could be seen for miles, and
would look out over all the surrounding fields that also belonged to the
castle's owner. In recent years it has been used as the setting for
many films and television programmes, including "Robin Hood", "Doctor
Who", "Sherlock Holmes" and "The Chronicles of Narnia".

*Escape route: (not suitable for pushchairs) to cut a sizeable
portion from the walk bear left along the driveway of Peckforton
Castle, then follow the signed footpath straight ahead. On the
other side of the hill bear left at the crossroads of footpaths,
signed for Burwardsley. Continue from Direction 16. Be warned
though this route goes over the hill – the full route goes round it,
but this gets you off the road.*

**12. Continue along the lane after Peckforton Lodge for just under
half a mile. Then bear left along a driveway to the left. (This is
signed as a private road. This applies only to vehicles – it is a
public footpath).**

☺ You should now have good views over to Beeston Castle, standing on the
top of a rocky crag. It is much older than Peckforton Castle and was
built nearly 800 years ago by the Sixth Earl of Chester. The castle is
supposed to have buried treasure hidden in its grounds, probably down
the very deep well, but no-one has ever found it.

**13. Avoid the footpaths to the right and continue ahead with the
trackway.**

Peckforton Cottage In The Snow

☺ There are still good views over to Beeston Castle. In 1642, during the
Civil War (when the government were fighting against King Charles I)
it was the scene of much fighting and was badly damaged, which is how
we see it today. It is now one of Cheshire's most visited historical
monuments.

> Q: The next building you pass on the right is called Moat House
>   Barn, which is on the right. It has two round windows looking out
>   over this driveway. On a building behind the house is another
>   weather vane. What animal does this one have on it?
> A: A cockerel

14. Bear left through the metal kissing gate along the wide
trackway through trees, leading slightly uphill onto the
Peckforton estate, signed for Burwardsley.

☺ These woods are part of the grounds of Peckforton Castle. There is a
Fire Warning on the left, because in very hot weather fires can easily

be started in woods, especially if there are dry leaves and twigs on the ground. There are many different types of trees here, including oak, holly and sweet chestnut. Sweet chestnut trees have long leaves with jagged edges, and are related to the Horse Chestnut.

Q: Do you know what the fruit of the Horse Chestnut tree is called? You have probably seen them many times.

A: Conkers

Keep a look out on the ground for fircones and see if you can tell which trees they have fallen from. In some places along the path you will be able to see between the trees (ON THE RIGHT) across the flat Cheshire Plain towards the hills of Wales.

15. At the crossroads of footpaths continue ahead, signed for Burwardsley.

☺ You may still see holes in the sandy banks along the path, which might have been made by rabbits or foxes. Soon you will pass a conifer plantation on the right. See if you can tell the difference between these trees and most of the other trees in the woods around you. The conifers have dark needles instead of leaves and they have tall, straight trunks or boughs, and they grow a lot quicker than most British trees.

  They are often grown for their wood, to make furniture or paper, and are also used as Christmas trees. Fir, pine and larch are all different types of conifers.

16. At the next junction keep with the main trackway, signed for The Pheasant Inn, leading downhill.

☺ If you walk quietly you may see squirrels on the ground looking for food. For some way the path is shaded by overhanging trees. Perhaps there are squirrels moving in the branches above you. Unless you are very quiet, the chances are they will see you before you see them.

  There are also many rabbits in the area. At some places along the path there are sandy banks with rabbit holes in them. Like squirrels, wild rabbits are shy creatures, and they will most probably be able to hear you approach and will dart for cover.

17. Follow the path as it leads downhill through overhanging trees and go through the gate at the end of the drive.

☺ Q: What is the name of the first farm on the right?
A: Spring House Farm

18. Continue ahead along the lane.

☺ Q: What is the name of a number of burrows where several rabbits live?
A: A warren. On the hill on the right there are many rabbit holes in the soft, sandy soil. There are also gorse bushes which have long prickles and yellow flowers. Hares are related to rabbits, but much larger. They tend to live in the middle of thick bushes, like gorse.

Q: On the left is a cottage made partly of sandstone. It is named after a flower. What is it called?
A: Lilac Cottage

19. Keep to the lane, avoiding footpaths on both sides, arriving at The Pheasant Inn on the left.

There are tables outside, including a patio with fine views for miles, a fountain and, of special interest to children, a playground and a telescope looking out over the Cheshire Plain. The Inn is very popular with walkers doing the Sandstone Trail.

☺ Q: What is pictured on the inn sign?
A: A Pheasant, which is a type of bird

The Pheasant Inn is very old, and has been running as a pub for at least 350 years, though it wasn't called the Pheasant until more recently. There have been many additions to the original building over the years, perhaps you can tell which are the newer parts.

Q: If you look carefully at the walls, you might notice some of them are decorated by models of a certain type of insect. What are they called?
A: Butterflies. Some of them are almost hidden in the ivy

20. Continue past the Pheasant Inn. At the crossroads go straight over, signed for the candle workshops. Follow the Barracks Lane uphill, the Sandstone Trail car park should be in a short way on the right.

Peckforton Checklist

☐	A CASTLE	☐	A RED CAR
☐	A STREAM	☐	A TRACTOR
☐	A RABBIT'S BURROW	☐	A SQUIRREL
☐	A TELESCOPE	☐	A STONE BRIDGE
☐	A COW	☐	A THATCHED COTTAGE
☐	AN ELEPHANT	☐	A STONE ARCHWAY

21. Redesmere and Capesthorne

This walk is entirely flat and includes some of the Cheshire Plain's most popular attractions. Redesmere has a wide variety of birdlife, so don't forget to bring some brown bread. Capesthorne Hall is one of the county's most impressive stately homes and is open to the public at weekends in summer, and occasional days throughout the week.

For info and opening times for Capesthorne Hall visit www.capesthorne.com or tel: 01625 861221

Starting point	**Car park at Redesmere Lake, Siddington. (SJ848713) off the A34 between Congleton and Alderley Edge**
By bus	**From Macclesfield, Manchester, Northwich and Knutsford to Monk's Heath. From here it is a mile and a half walk along the roadside footpath**
Distance	**3 miles**
Terrain	**Flat all the way over fields and along lanes. Possibly some mud in wet weather**
Maps	**OS Landranger 118**
Public Toilets	**None. (The public toilets near Redesmere, marked on some OS maps have now been demolished)**
Refreshments	**Tea Room at Capesthorne Hall, for visitors only**
Pushchairs	**Not suitable**

1. At the car park lay-by face the lake then turn right, so the lake is on your left, and follow the lane alongside the lake.

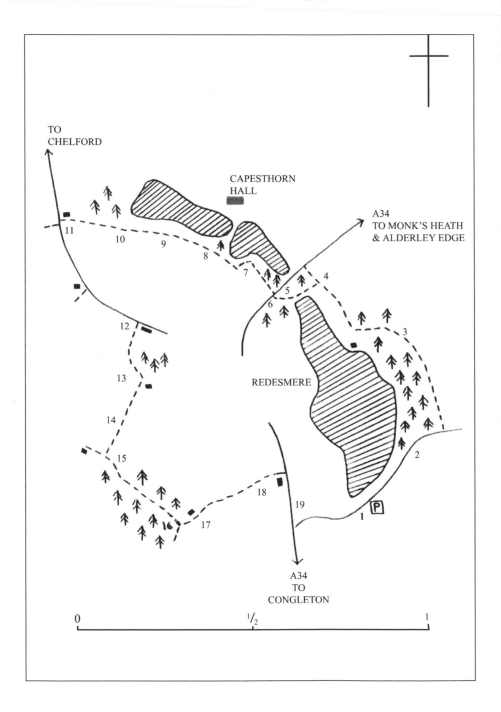

TO
CHELFORD

CAPESTHORN
HALL

A34
TO MONK'S HEATH
& ALDERLEY EDGE

11

10   9

8

7

6   5   4

3

12

13

REDESMERE

14

2

15

18   19   1

17

16

A34
TO
CONGLETON

0   ½   1

Redesmere is a well-known local beauty spot with ample parking along its southern shore. There are good views across the lake.

☺ The Lake is called Redesmere, which means quite simply "reedy lake". There are many birds here including swans, mallards, coots, herons and Canada geese. Perhaps you can recognise some of them?

2. **Pass an area of woodland on the left after the lake – avoid gates or stiles into the woods. Take the stile on the left after the woods along a signed public footpath across an open field. Climb a further stile and continue ahead along a fenced path with the woods on your left.**

☺ There may be horses or donkeys grazing in this field. Donkeys get lonely if they are left by themselves, so they are often kept in pairs, or with a horse companion.

3. **Climb the stile at the end of the footpath and bear left along the trackway, through bushes and tall reeds. Cross the wooden bridge over a stream. Go through the gate and pass the yacht club on the left, then join the stony trackway. Follow it along the length of the lake. (Alternatively follow the edge of the lake.)**

☺ Q: What shape is the flag on the sign at the gate of the Yacht Club?
   A: Triangular (the sign is in the hedge to the right of the gate)

4. **At the end of the lake bear left over the grass and cross a small footbridge. Continue along the path which runs along the foot of the lake.**

☺ There are good views from here along the lake towards the yacht club. Perhaps there are boats or windsurfers on the water. There are many reeds and bulrushes growing in the shallow water around the edge of the lake. The long brown part of the bulrush contains hundreds of tiny seeds, which get blown away by the wind to hopefully find somewhere to grow.

5. **Continue over another footbridge and follow the path to the main road.**

☺ The stream is the overflow from Redesmere. After heavy rain the lake will be fuller and more water will flow out in this stream. The water goes from here into a series of further lakes which you will soon come to.

6. **Cross the road, taking care as there are bends in both directions. Follow the path across the field opposite, signed for Mill Lane, running along the edge of a farmed field, with the woods on your right.**

☺ The path runs around the edge of a farmed field. Sometimes the field may be grass, or sometimes a crop, such as wheat, which Cheshire is famous for. In the woods (ON THE RIGHT) there are many wild animals, such as rabbits and hares and possibly foxes and badgers. Keep your eyes open and you might see one, though they tend to keep well away from people. Notice how the trees nearest the fence are smaller than those behind. They are younger and have not yet fully grown.

7. **Approach the first pond with the boathouse on the opposite bank, and bear left to the stile. After the stile keep right, passing the pond and coming to a further lake, over which is Capesthorne Hall.**

☺ These lakes are not natural, but were made by damming the stream that runs out of Redesmere, so that the water flooded the lowest parts of the fields. This was done by the people who lived at Capesthorne Hall over the lake. You may be able to see (ON THE OPPOSITE SIDE OF THE WATER, TOWARDS THE BEGINNING OF THE LAKE) a brick and stone column, like a tall gatepost, standing in the middle of the field. This is to mark the spot where the old hall used to stand before it was demolished and the present house was built.
     Capesthorne Hall is the home of the Bromley-Davenport family, who were wealthy landowners (and are still quite well-off, for that matter). The hall is built of brick with various turrets and towers to decorate it. Its front is longer than the Queen's home, Buckingham Palace. The oldest part of Capesthorne is almost 280 years old and is at the back. The rest of the house was destroyed by fire and had to be rebuilt. It looks very grand in daylight, but at night, beware, for the hall is said to

be haunted! A mysterious Lady in Grey roams through the rooms and along the dark corridors of the old building...

Forty years ago when a member of the family, William Bromley-Davenport, was in bed, he was awoken by a sound; a scratching at his window. He opened the curtains and to his horror he saw a hand hanging in mid-air, with the fingers scraping at the glass. When he very bravely opened the window the hand disappeared, and has never appeared again, but the tale has not been forgotten.

8. Continue along the lake towards the ornamental bridge.

☺ Q: How many arches are there on the bridge?
  A: Five

9. Go through the kissing gate and continue along the lakeside.

☺ Over the water you can see the side of the Hall and the gardens. The pathway between the lawns leads to the Hall's private chapel where there is a family crypt where the Bromley-Davenport family have been buried for years. Another haunting takes place there, as a line of ghostly figures has been seen gliding silently down the steps into the crypt.

10. Continue past the lake and follow the gravel trackway. Climb the stile and continue ahead to the lane.

☺ In the trees (ON THE RIGHT) is the old saw mill (now used by "Dinghycraft"). It was worked until 1936 using waterpower to turn the circular cutting saw. It provided all the wood for the estate, for fences and buildings.

11. Bear left along mill lane. (Wide grass verges on both sides.)

☺ (AT PARK FARM, ON THE BEND OF THE LANE.) This is Park Farm, and was at one time part of the Capesthorne Estate, and would have grown crops for the family who lived at the Hall. Above the door is the family coat of arms, or emblem.

12. Avoid the footpath on the right after the farm, continue along the lane, which bears around to the left. Take the stile on the

right just before the brick cottages. Cross the field - with your back to the lane - towards the woods. Climb the stile and continue with the woods on your left.

☺ These are mixed woods, and have many different types of trees. Some of the trees have berries. Elderberries have purple/black clusters of small berries in the late summer and early autumn. Rowans have lots of bright orange berries that turn red in the autumn. Hawthorns also have red berries and sharp prickles. They provide winter food for the birds, when there is little else around for them to eat.

13. Climb the stile in the wire fence, continue ahead to a further stile in the hedge. Cross over and bear left across the field. As you round the edge of the woods a farmhouse should come into view. The next stile is to the right of the house.

☺ (AT THE STILE) To the right is a small pond with many overhanging trees, surrounded by rushes and reeds. There may be ducks here. Ducks have flat "webbed" feet, which act like flippers and help them swim. The female ducks are usually a brown colour, while the males are more colourful, with green and blue patterns on their feathers. See if you can tell the difference between them.

14. Climb the stile and keep right, around the small pond, then follow the path along the edge of the field, with the hedge on your right.

☺ (A SHORT WAY ACROSS THE FIELD INDICATE TO THE RIGHT) Over the flat fields you should be able to see what looks like a huge satellite dish. This is the Jodrell Bank Radio Telescope, but it isn't a telescope that you can look through. The dish points to the sky and listens to radio waves.

   It can track objects moving in space, like comets, rockets and UFOs...

15. Keep straight ahead along the field edge. Climb the stile at the end of the field and bear left along a grassy trackway. In a short way the track is barred by a five bar gate, but the footpath continues to the right of the gate along the edge of some woodland.

A gaggle of geese at Redesmere

☺ This path is also used by horse riders. See if you can see any hoof-prints on the ground.

    A stream runs through the woods, down in the trees to the right. You may be able to hear the rushing of its water.

16. **Where the path divides bear left and keep to the main track-way, leading slightly uphill.**

☺ There is a house on the left through the trees with a thatched roof; that is a roof made of straw. Thatched roofs sometimes have to be replaced and the person who does this job is called a "thatcher". It has now become a name, like baker, woodman and so on. Perhaps you have heard the name Thatcher before?

17. **Pass the buildings on the left and bear right along the rutted driveway.**

☺ Look at the fields. Some will probably be grass, but others may have wheat or corn in them.

> Q: What food is made from wheat, that most people eat nearly every day?
> A: Bread. Also breakfast cereals, biscuits and many other things

18. At the head of the drive pass farm buildings and bear right along the footpath of the main road.

☺ (ON THE LEFT AT THE TOP OF THE LANE) This is the remains of what was once an orchard. There are many fruit trees, including damsons with large purple fruit, used for making jam and wine. There are also elderberry trees and blackberry bushes.

(ON THE ROAD) Here there are more thatched cottages with white-painted brick walls.

> Q: How many chimneys can you count on the cottages?
> A: Four

19. Avoid the left turning for the village hall, take the next left turning along Redesmere Lane. Take care on the lane and while crossing the main road. The lane leads in a short distance back to the car park at Redesmere.

There are picnic tables on the left before the lake, in an enclosed area that once contained the public toilets. At the start of the lake there is a notice board with pictures of all the bird types that visit Redesmere.

Redesmere and Capesthorne Checklist

☐ A SILVER CAR	☐ A BOAT OR WINDSURFER
☐ A SWAN	☐ A DUCK
☐ A HORSE	☐ A COW
☐ BULRUSHES	☐ A WOODEN FOOTBRIDGE
☐ A STONE BRIDGE	☐ A TREE WITH BERRIES
☐ A BLACKBERRY BUSH	☐ A THATCHED ROOF

Other places of interest in the area

Jodrell Bank Radio Telescope And Science Centre
Well signed from the A535 between Chelford and Holmes Chapel. Working models of the radio telescope, planetarium, displays and exhibitions, attractive arboretum in the grounds, child friendly science "games", cafe and toilets. open daily throughout most of the year.

For more information check out their website: www.jodrellbank.manchester.ac.uk

22. Risley Moss

Risley Moss is a nature reserve on the outskirts of Warrington. It was once the site of a munitions factory and peat was later cut from the area. Since then the Moss has been purposely waterlogged to encourage moss growth and wetland birds and insects. It is a haven for such wildlife and therefore an essential port of call for any amateur or junior naturalists. There is a Visitor Centre packed with information, helpful wardens on hand and various woodland hides, and it's all free! An excellent place to have a picnic, with picnic tables at various locations. Please note though, that the Moss is closed on Fridays.

For information/opening times visit www.warrington.gov.uk and put Risley Moss in the search box, or phone 01925 824339.

Starting point	Risley Moss Local Nature Reserve (SJ665920) which can be found a mile from junction 11 of the M62, just north-east of Warrington
By rail	Nearest station: Birchwood, on the Manchester to Liverpool line. It is then a walk of just over a mile
Distance	Entire route: a mere mile!
Terrain	Flat gravel paths through woodland. Suitable for any weather
Maps	OS landranger 109. Also map of reserve available from Visitor Centre
Public Toilets	At the Visitor Centre
Refreshments	None in the immediate area
Pushchairs	An ideal circular route along well maintained paths

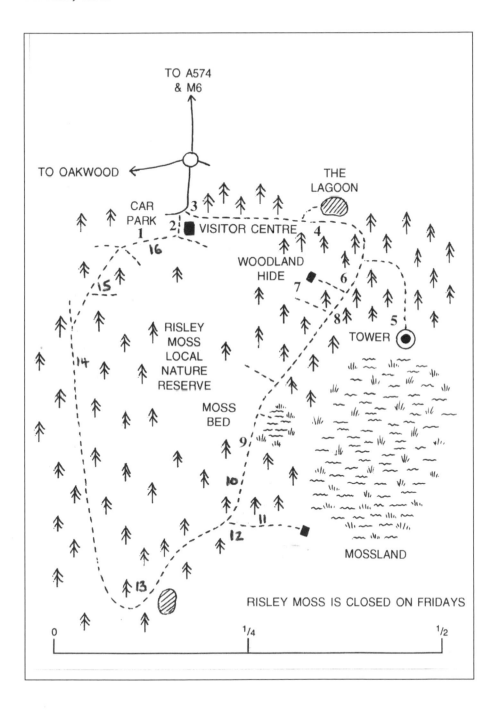

TO A574 & M6

TO OAKWOOD ←

THE LAGOON

CAR PARK

VISITOR CENTRE

WOODLAND HIDE

RISLEY MOSS LOCAL NATURE RESERVE

TOWER

MOSS BED

MOSSLAND

RISLEY MOSS IS CLOSED ON FRIDAYS

0   1/4   1/2

1. **Once through the main gates of the reserve (the car park is well signed) follow the paths to the Visitor Centre, visible through the trees.**

☺ This is the Visitor Centre. Inside there is information about the birds, insects and animals that you might see on your walk. On the wall of the centre there are large models of a dragonfly, frog, kingfisher and several other animals. How many can you recognise?

2. **Facing the Visitor Centre, bear left and then right, around the side of the centre.**

3. **Take the first left turning, passing the picnic site on your right. The path curves, passing the pedestrian exit.**

☺ This is a mixed wood, meaning it has different types of trees growing in it. Here they are mainly oak and ash trees, but there are also beech and prickly hawthorns.

4. **Keep to the main path at all times. Avoid the steps to the left and continue past the pond.**

☺ On the left is a viewing point over a small pond with duckweed floating on its surface, and rushes, brambles and reeds around its banks, which attract many insects like dragonflies and butterflies.
   Further along the path there are many logs left amongst the trees to "decay". Rotten tree trunks provide homes for thousands of insects, which can burrow into the soft, dead wood. Some of the tree trunks will probably have fungus growing on them.

5. **At the junction bear left, signed for the tower. (The path bears around to the right – the left turning is private.)**

☺ Wait... what's that... through the trees? A strange object looking somewhat like a UFO. This is an observation tower. If you climb the steps into the tower there are views across an area of pools, swamps and undergrowth, which is called "mossland". This is land that has been waterlogged by building many ditches, and stopping rainwater from draining away, so the soil is always wet. This makes the ground ideal for mosses and other plants that like a lot of moisture. The trees have been removed from the area, as they would "drink" a lot of the water. Trees drink through their roots, which can spread under the ground for a very long way. A birch tree can absorb 30 gallons of water a day. That's 240 pints, which is about the same as two baths full almost to the top. The mossland attracts a lot of birds, butterflies and many other insects.

6. **Return the same way, keeping left and the minor junction, then left again at the main junction, signed for the Woodland Hide.**

☺ In this part of the woods there are many trees which have berries in the late summer and autumn. See if you can see any. Elderberry trees have clusters of small black/purple berries. Rowans have many bright red berries. The berries contain seeds, which are carried away by birds and from which a new tree could grow.

7. **Take the next right turning, signed for the Woodland Hide.**

☺ This path leads to a "hide". This is a special building where you can sit inside and look out at wild animals and birds, without them seeing you. It is quite dark inside the hide. If you go in, keep quiet, so you do not disturb other people who might be trying to watch the animals. If you sit for a short while, see if you can see any animals, like birds or squirrels. Food is put out to attract birds to this area.

8. **Return the same way and bear right along the main path. Keep straight at the junction, signed for the Mossland Hide.**

   Escape route: take the next right turning, signed for the Visitor Centre.

9. **Continue ahead along the main path, signed for the Mossland Hide. Avoid minor turnings.**

☺ Look out for a wooden walkway to the left, where you can look over an area of moss, called spagnum moss. It grows well in wet conditions. The mossland you could see from the tower is made up mainly of this type of moss.

10. Continue ahead along the main path.

☺ Many of the trees along the path here are very thin, because they are growing very close together. There are many other plants in the woods, like nettles, which can sting you, blackberry bushes, which have sharp prickles, and on the ground you might see toadstools and mushrooms, especially in the autumn. Never touch or eat wild berries or mushrooms, as they might be very poisonous. Many birds and small animals eat the fruit and berries from trees, but that doesn't mean they are alright for people to eat.

11. Bear left, signed for the Mossland Hide.

☺ This is another hide, like the one you visited earlier. The other hide looked out into the woodlands. This hide looks over the mossland, over ferns and water. Many different types of birds can be seen from here. Some of the more common ones are magpies, ducks and gulls. Also look for herons, which have long legs and can wade through water. Sit quietly for a few minutes and see how many birds you can see.

12. Return to the main path and bear left.

☺ You should soon pass another small pond on the left. Again this has green weeds on the surface on the water, and many reeds around its edges. Perhaps there are birds or insects near the water.

13. Follow the path as it bears around to the right.

☺ This part of the woods has many silver birch trees. They have slim, silvery white trunks and diamond shaped leaves. There are often red-capped toadstools growing under birch trees.

   There are many holly bushes amongst the trees in this area. Holly has prickly leaves – can you think of any other plants that have prickles? Holly is an evergreen – which means it keeps

Risley Moss observation tower

its leaves throughout the winter. Can you think of any other evergreen plants? (Fir trees, ivy and rhododendrons are some – there are some rhododendron bushes later on – they have large white, pink or lilac flowers in the spring.)

14. Look out for the junction for the "Minimoss Trail" - push-chairs continue along the main path, leading slightly uphill at this point.

As an optional detour follow the sign for the Minimoss Trail, leading you between swamps and overhanging trees. Keep right, up the steps and bear left along the main path to the Visitor Centre.

15. Keep straight ahead, soon the Visitor Centre should come into view ahead.

☺ You have probably noticed several wooden sculptures on your walk around Risley Moss. These are carved from fallen logs; many of them are in the shape of local animals. How many have you spotted?

16. Pass the Visitor Centre on your right and bear left for the main car park.

Risley Moss Checklist

☐ A WOODEN OWL	☐ A SQUIRREL
☐ A POND	☐ A BIRD'S FEATHER
☐ A BLACKBERRY BUSH	☐ A WOODEN BENCH
☐ A PERSON WALKING A DOG	☐ A PICNIC TABLE
☐ A DUCK	☐ A FALLEN TREE OR LOG

23. Shining Tor

Again, another area that is wild, dramatic and isolated; surely one of the most remote areas of the county. The ascent of Shining Tor is a steady but quite straightforward climb to spectacular views in any season – but wrap up warm!

Starting point	Pym Chair car park (SJ995768) from Macclesfield follow signs for Buxton, then Goyt Valley. Pass Jenkin Chapel on the corner at Saltersford, follow the road uphill, then bear left before the descent into the Goyt Valley. The car park is on the right
By bus	Nearest bus service is to Kettleshule from Macclesfield
Distance	4 miles, with no escape routes
Terrain	Moorland paths and farm trackways. A steady, but not difficult climb to the summit
Maps	OS Landranger 118 OS Outdoor Leisure 24
Public Toilets	None along the route. The nearest are in the Goyt Valley, across the dam, or the car park and picnic area at Lamaload Reservoir
Refreshments	Nearest place is the Tea Cosy Cafe, on the Main Road in Kettleshulme, open Friday to Monday. Closed in January
Pushchairs	Not suitable at all

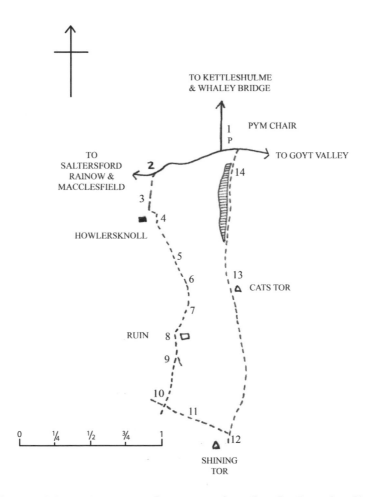

1. **At the road junction near the car park, take the lane leading steeply downhill.**

2. **Then take the footpath on the left, along a farm driveway, leading downhill.**

☺ The drive leads downhill, and goes over a small stream. There are many trees around the water, and also prickly thistles, which can grow quite tall and in the summer have purple flowers. They are the emblem for Scotland, and are shown on some pound coins.

You should soon see the farmhouse ahead along the driveway. It is made of stone, and has what look like two X's on the front of it. Do you know what these are for? They aren't because someone is learning the alphabet either. They are the ends of supports which help stop the walls of the house collapsing. You can often see them on old buildings.

3. **Go through the gate across the track and continue down to the farmhouse. Go through the wooden gate on the left directly before the farmhouse. Climb the ladder stile on the right.**

☺ Q: There should be hens on the right in the garden of the farmhouse. Hens are female. Do you know what the male is called?

A: A cockerel

4. **Continue ahead, passing the farmhouse. Climb the next stile and follow the track uphill to the left.**

The ascent to Cat's Tor

☺ There may be the occasional rabbit hole, or much smaller holes made by mice or voles. There should soon be views downhill to the right into the steep-sided valley.

5. **Cross through the stream then go through an open gateway – here leave the track and bear right with the drystone wall on your right.**

   NB: the paths can be difficult to follow from now on, but basically you want to be aiming for the head of the valley.

6. **Keep straight ahead, eventually going through another gateway – keep ahead across the open field to the stile.**

☺ Have you noticed there are no trees now? There is only grass, kept short by the sheep and cows. As well as the normal grass, there is also marram grass, which grows along the many small streams that run down into the valley.

   You may see small mounds of soil made by moles. Moles are small and mouse-like, except they have big paws which they use as shovels for digging their holes. They live underground and are very short-sighted.

7. **Climb the stile and continue ahead to a further stile, crossing several small streams.**

☺ There are no houses or trees in sight now. This could seem a very lonely place if you were by yourself, but some people like this kind of loneliness, when they can get away from the town and all the pollution and come for a walk, perhaps not meeting anybody at all.

   In the mud on the ground see if you can see any boot prints, or the prints left by animals, like cows or horses. Can you guess which print belongs to which animal? Cows have two "toes", while horses' hoof prints should show the shape of their horseshoes.

   Soon you should come to a ruined house. You can see the old gateposts and the crumbling stone walls. Do not go too near, as the walls are unsafe. Never climb on old walls like these as they are likely to collapse on top of you.

8. **The path comes round to the right of an old ruin and leads to a stile. Climb this and bear right and cross the stream. Follow**

the path uphill, cross the stile and continue ahead.

9.   When the path splits, keep right, continuing uphill. It soon crosses a broken wall, and shortly after goes through another. That was the tricky bit. It is easy to follow from now on. There should be a fence and partially broken wall on your right. Continue uphill with the wall.

☺ On your left there should be a steep valley with a small stream in it. This is the beginning of Todd Brook, which you saw earlier. It collects all the rainwater that drains from the surrounding hills, and takes it all to the Toddbrook Reservoir.

10. Climb the stile and continue ahead, cross a further stile and continue ahead. At the top avoid the various stiles and bear left, with the wall and fence on your right.

☺ Over on the right, in the distance, you should be able to see the unmistakable outline of Shutlingsloe, a hill, which from here is triangular, or pyramid shaped. Down below there is a road, which is the first sign of civilisation for some way.

11. Follow the path as it begins the final climb. At the top climb the stile and bear right, signed for "The Cat and Fiddle". After a very short way there is another stile on the right, which will take you to the trig point, that being the top of Shining Tor.

☺ (AT THE TRIG POINT) This is Shining Tor, which is on the border between the counties of Cheshire and Derbyshire. The white stone monument shows that it is the highest point in the area. Below there are fields and farms, and views in the distance towards the Cheshire Plain.

12. From the Trig Point return over the stile and bear left. Follow the fence and wall all the way, straight ahead.

☺ It is fairly flat on the top, and used to be quite muddy, until these stone slabs were put down to make a path, so you don't have to get your feet wet and muddy. The black mud you can see around you is called peat, which is a type of soil, which at one time was cut into strips and could be burnt on fires. This isn't that common now, as peat-cutting was damaging miles of countryside.

The only plants growing in the peat are heather and bilberries. Both grow close to the ground and can survive the cold, wet weather and strong winds. Heather has tiny flowers of white, pink, purple or red. It is often used in gardens for rockeries, because it keeps its colours all the year round. Bilberries have light green, oval leaves, and purple-black berries in the autumn. The fruit is sometimes used for making jam or wine.

13. **The path ascends to Cat Tor, then drops down all the way back to Pym Chair.**

☺ Over on the right there are views into Derbyshire and towards the Goyt Valley. The moorland along the path is a "Conservation Area", which means it is a place where the plants can grow without getting trampled on or damaged, and where animals can live safely. Do not stray from the path, as there might be birds nesting on the ground, which you would disturb and frighten.

Eventually there is a slight climb and you should be able to see rocky crags ahead on the left. Soon there should be views down to the Goyt Forest on the right, unless it's very misty, and then you won't see a thing.

After a short way it is all downhill, and not far from the end of the walk.

14. **At the end of the path go through the gate and descend to the road. Bear left and then right to the car park. There are verges and paths alongside the edge of the road.**

☺ Here we are, back at Pym Chair – look out for the sign telling you about Pym – who was believed to be either a highwayman who hid in the rocks waiting to rob people, or a priest who delivered sermons from the rocks.

Shining Tor Checklist

☐	A STONE FARMHOUSE	☐	A JOGGER
☐	A DOG	☐	A SHEEP
☐	A HANG GLIDER	☐	A WHITE CAR
☐	A WHITE HORSE	☐	HEATHER
☐	A STREAM	☐	SOMEONE WEARING A HAT
☐	A STONE RUIN	☐	A WOODEN BENCH

24. Styal Woods

An excellent day out for children, especially if a visit to the Mill is included. Along the River Bollin there are easy walks through attractive mixed woodland, carefully maintained by The National Trust. Ideal for any season.

For info: www.nationaltrust.org.uk put Styal or Quarry Bank Mill in the search box. Tel: 01625 445896 (Infoline) or 01625 527468

Starting point	**National Trust car park near Norcliffe Chapel, (SJ835835) off Altrincham Road, Styal**
By rail	**Styal Station. Bear right for Styal Village**
Distance	**Entire route 3 miles, many Escape Routes, can be made into two short walks of a mile and a half each**
Terrain	**Well maintained pathways through the woods. Some uphill stretches**
Maps	**OS Landrangers 109**
Public Toilets	**Quarry Bank Mill**
Refreshments	**Quarry Bank Mill**
Pushchairs	**The whole route would be difficult if not impossible for pushchairs, though there is good accessibility around the village and the mill area. The Western Woods are acceptable with some effort. A short and pleasant circuit of the Southern Woods can be made from the car park at Twinnies Bridge, off Styal Road (SJ839822)**

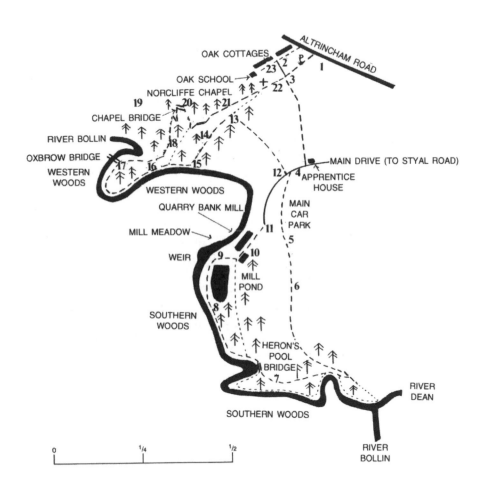

1. **From the National Trust car park turn right along Altrincham Road, passing allotments on the right, then bear right along the cobbled driveway that leads to Norcliffe Chapel.**

☺ Over 200 years ago, an Irishman called Samuel Greg built a cotton mill nearby on the banks of the River Bollin. He later built homes for his workers, (FARM FOLD COTTAGES ON THE LEFT) like these simple, but well-kept cottages.

☺ A short way ahead in an enclosure on the left is a headless cross. This is Styal Cross, believed to be at least 500 years old. It used to stand near the main road, but was damaged in a road accident and its remains were eventually moved here, where they would be safe from further damage.

2. **Directly after the cross bear left through the gate; follow the footpath and pass a small pond.**

☺ Over on the left are more cottages, which were made from a large barn to house the increasing number of mill workers. The building with a lantern over the door is Styal Chapel and was at one time a farm building where grain was stored. It was made into a church over 150 years ago.

3. **Continue straight across at the "crossroads" of paths and follow the footpath.**

The fields on either side of the path are leased to farmers by the National Trust and dairy cows can often be seen here.

☺ Q: What are black and white cows called?
   A: Freisians

☺ (THE WHITE BUILDING VISIBLE AHEAD AND TO THE LEFT) This is the Apprentice House. Local orphans were brought to work in the mill, and this building was where they lived. They ranged from nine to eighteen years old, and in return for their work they were fed and clothed and received a basic education. Their lives, though much better than in the workhouses, were hard, and they worked long hours in the mill, from six o'clock in the morning until seven o'clock at night. The

Apprentice House was home to an average of 85 children at any one time, and they slept in large rooms with the girls on one side and the boys on the other.

Escape route: bear right along the drive and take the second footpath on the right, signed "To The Woods" then follow Directions 13 and onwards.

4. **Bear right along the driveway for a short way, then go through the gap in the wall on the left, which leads to the main car park. Follow the path, with the cars on your left.**

☺ (LARGE IRON AXLE ON THE GRASS ON THE RIGHT) This was part of the giant waterwheel from the mill that used the power of water to turn the mill machinery. A new wheel has now taken its place.

Escape route: follow the path to the right, downhill to Quarry Bank Mill, where there are toilets, shop, café. Continue from Direction 11.

5. **Continue along the path to the far side of the car park, passing a small pond on the right. Go through the gate straight ahead, cross over the rutted trackway and continue onto farmed land. Keep straight ahead with the hedge on your right.**

☺ This path is known as the Apprentices' Path, because the children from the Apprentice House would walk along here to the church in Wilmslow every Sunday morning.
   Notice how the hedge (ON THE RIGHT) is made up of many different plants, which have all grown together. This hedge is mainly hawthorn, (which has sharp thorns), but there are also brambles, (with prickly stems) and holly (which has prickly leaves). Hedges like these make ideal places for wild animals to

Woodland walk, Styal Woods

shelter and build nests.

Manchester Airport is close by and you may see and hear many planes taking off and landing.

6. **Go through the five bar gate and follow the pathway between fences and hedge. At the end of the path go through the iron kissing gate and continue ahead, downhill. Keep right, going through a metal gate into Styal Woods. Keep right, along Bluebell Bank.**

☺ (A SHORT WAY INTO THE WOODS) There are many willow trees in this part of the woods. They have many long, thin leaves. See if you can spot any. They were grown here for their long, stem-like branches.

Q: Can you guess what for?
A: They were made into baskets

7. **After a quarter of a mile, take the path uphill and cross Heron's Pool Bridge and continue ahead along the main path.**

☺ The river here is wide and slow, and often a brown colour, from the sandy mud it carries with it. In many places the bank has had to be shored up, to prevent it from collapsing into the river, as the water steadily wears it away.

8. **Bear left at the junction, so the mill pond is on your right.**

Escape route: to cut off a short way avoid the left turning and continue ahead – keep along the main path all the way to the mill. Continue from Direction 10.

Take care of the mill pond, river and especially the up-coming weir.

☺ This pond was at one time used to store water which would be used to turn the waterwheel inside the mill. It is now a haven for wildlife, with bulrushes growing along its banks. How many birds or ducks you can see.

☺ The large building ahead is Quarry Bank Mill, a cotton mill. Cotton comes from a plant, and when it is harvested it is in fluffy white balls like cotton wool. These balls can be spun to make yarn (thick threads) which can then be made into clothes. The mill was built 200 years ago. Underneath it is a large waterwheel, which is turned by the water from the River Bollin. The wheel was able to power the mill machines and make them work, before electricity was invented.

☺ You can probably hear the great rushing of water from ahead. (ON THE BEND OF THE PATH, ON THE LEFT) This is the weir, which is used to control the level of water, so that there is always enough to power the waterwheel.

9. **Continue along the path around the mill pond, cross the bridge and bear left onto the main path towards the mill.**

☺ (THE STREAM RUNNING ON THE LEFT OF THE MAIN PATH) This stream is called the "head race", which is a channel of water taken from the main river which runs into the mill to the waterwheel. (FROM THE MAIN PATH, SHORTLY BEFORE THE STEPS THAT LEAD DOWN TO THE MILL) Here you can see a "lock-gate" which can be raised or lowered to adjust the flow of water to the mill. To stop the waterwheel from turning, the lock gate can be lowered, which stops the flow of water. The other gate opposite can be opened and the water will flow back to the river.

You should shortly pass a small children's playground on the left before the final descent to the mill yard.

10. **Go down the steep steps into the cobbled courtyard by the mill buildings.**

Here you will find the entrance to Quarry Bank Mill, a working museum which attracts thousands of visitors from all over the country. Inside there are displays relating to the story of cotton production and the chance to see the mill in action, with constantly clacking looms and spinning machines. It may not be suitable for very young children, but most youngsters find it quite interesting as long as parents don't linger too long. Many local schools do projects about the mill and the history of the cotton industry, so any information gleaned now might come in useful in years to come. Tickets are available from the reception on the right, near the National Trust shop. To the left is the Mill Kitchen Cafe and Restaurant, and the public toilets.

   For a better view of the weir, or to picnic, follow the path directly in front of the mill and bear left along a cobbled track to the mill meadow.

11. From the mill continue along the main driveway, leading uphill.

☺ The mill is much larger today than when it was first built, as business was going so well that it was possible to extend the building several times. On the roof there is a small bell-tower. The bell was used to call the villagers to work in the morning. In many mill villages someone would have to go around knocking on all the doors to wake everyone up for work, because no-one had an alarm clock.

Escape route: bear right up the slope or steps to return to the main car park.

☺ (ON THE LEFT SHORTLY AFTER THE MILL IS THE GATEWAY TO A WHITE GEORGIAN HOUSE) This is Quarry Bank House, where Samuel Greg, the owner of the Mill lived with his family. While he was alive the mill was very successful and made great profits and he was able to open mills elsewhere. When he died his sons took over his business, but it was not as successful.

12. Take the footpath on the left, signed "To the Woods". Follow the path between hawthorn hedges, crossing a driveway at the middle point, and continue ahead into the woods, to a T-junction of paths.

Escape route: to return to the Altrincham Road car park, turn right here and keep straight ahead.

13. To continue with the route, bear left through the woods.

Beware of the drop down on the right!

☺ Q: There are many different types of trees and bushes in the woods. How many can you recognise?

A: Some of the more common varieties are:
         Rhododendron bushes
         Holly
         Beech
         Hawthorn
         Oak
         Sycamore

14. Follow the path and steps down to the river.

☺ Quarry Bank Mill is further along the river, and the water was used to
   turn a huge waterwheel which powered the mill machinery and weaved
   thread into cotton cloth. Perhaps you are wearing something made from
   cotton.

☺ Q: Does cotton come from an animal or a plant?
   A: Cotton comes from a plant and is in fluffy balls like cotton wool
          when it is harvested. It is then spun into threads and made into
          clothes

Chapel Bridge, Styal Woods

15. At the river bear right, crossing Kingfisher Bridge and continuing along the riverside path. When the path splits, keep left, close to the river. The path passes through an area of conifers.

☺ These tall trees are called conifers or evergreens.

Q: What is an evergreen tree?
A: They don't lose their leaves in winter like most British trees do, so they stay green all year round. They are often grown in forests for their wood to make furniture and paper.

16. Follow the path around the bend of the river.

☺ There are many birds and wild animals in the woods. If you keep very quiet and still for a few minutes you might see a squirrel running along the branches or on the ground looking for food. They build homes out of leaves and twigs. These are called dreys and look like large birds' nests. If you look high up in the trees, you might see a drey.

Q: What do you think squirrels eat?
A: They eat nuts and seeds from the trees, like acorns and fircones, young green shoots and sometimes steal birds' eggs and young chicks

17. Follow the path, passing a bridge on the left. Pass the bridge and continue through an area of tall conifers. Bear left uphill, partially stepped.

To extend the walk you can cross the bridge, which leads deeper into the woods, but there is no circular route.

☺ At the top of the hill, notice on the left a view across a farmed field to a further part of the woods where there are a variety of different trees of varying colours. In late spring and summer the trees are at their best. Many of them are from other countries and were planted by Greg's son, Robert.

18. Follow the path around a tight bend, through bushes and trees, passing on the right several redwoods with soft, flaking bark.

☺ These trees.are called Redwoods, because of the reddish colour of their bark. They grow very tall, and in America they have grown so big that holes have been made in the bottom of their trunks for cars to drive through.

19. The path soon bears downhill, zigzagging to a stone bridge.

☺ This is Chapel Bridge, built by Greg's son, Robert. These woods were originally the grounds of his house, nearby Norcliffe Hall. The small bridge further along the gully is a folly; an attractive showpiece. It is not safe to cross.

20. Go over Chapel Bridge and climb the steps leading uphill. Bear left up a further set of steps and then left onto the main path. In a short distance you should pass on the right a further bridge.

☺ This is the Centenary Bridge, built to celebrate the 100th anniversary of the National Trust, who own and care for this land and many other sites throughout Britain. It was opened on 26 July 1995.

21. Continue along the path, leaving the woods (passing an information board and map on the right). Continue alongside Norcliffe Chapel.

☺ The chapel is built of brick with a roof of stone slabs. If you look at the small belltower you may be able to see the bell, which called the villagers to church on Sunday mornings.

22. Continue to the centre of the village and take the cobbled driveway opposite the cross, leading between lawns towards estate cottages.

☺ These are further houses built by Greg for his workforce, and are called Oak Cottages. There was, on average, a family of eight people living in each cottage, which makes them very cramped by today's standards, but they were sheer luxury compared to the terrible conditions in the Manchester slums at the time. Each of the cottages had a small garden or allotment, so that some flowers and vegetables could be grown.

☺ The building at the end of the row (TO THE LEFT) is Oak School, which Greg built to educate his staff. Younger children came here during the day, and older children who worked in the mill came in the evenings or at week-ends. There were also classes for adults, as not all grown-ups could read and write.

Between the two rows of cottages, on the right, is a shop front with displays of old tins and food packages in its windows.

☺ This was the village shop, where the mill workers could buy their food, the cost of which would be deducted from their wages. The old tins and packets are very different from modern ones. Are there any you can recognise?

23. **Bear right along the path in front of the cottages. Continue past the allotments on the right, then bear right into the car park.**

Styal Woods and Quarry Bank Mill Checklist

☐	A BLACK AND WHITE COW	☐	A CHURCH SPIRE
☐	A SQUIRREL	☐	A FIRCONE
☐	A PLANE IN FLIGHT	☐	A WILD RABBIT
☐	IVY ON A TREE OR WALL	☐	A DUCK ON WATER
☐	A WOODEN BRIDGE	☐	A SACK OF SUGAR
☐	A TALL MILL CHIMNEY	☐	A RED CAR

25. Swettenham

Swettenham is a pleasant, sleepy village in an unspoilt and very rural area. It is rich, fertile farming country, and fields of corn and wheat are plentiful: the very essence of Cheshire. It is an area renowned for its wildlife along the banks of the River Dane and the Swettenham Brook Valley. The ideal place to get away from it all. Except for the occasional piece of farm machinery, it could be a century ago.

Starting point	The Swettenham Arms, Swettenham (SJ799672). The village is signed from the A535 Holmes Chapel to Chelford Road, and A34 Congleton to Alderley Edge Road and is situated just north of the River Dane. The pub is signed in the village, and is easy to find. It is situated directly behind the church. There are a few places around the lanes where parking is available for single cars. Please park sensibly and respect other road users and the villagers. There is parking at the Swettenham Arms for patrons only
By rail	Nearest stations: Holmes Chapel and Goostrey. Both have a series of footpaths which can be used to reach Swettenham without using roads
Distance	Entire circular route from Swettenham Arms: 3 miles
Terrain	Except for a brief climb after crossing Swettenham Brook, the route is entirely flat, using mainly footpaths along fields and farm trackways
Maps	OS Landrangers 118

Public Toilets	Nearest public toilets are at Brereton Heath Park. There are toilets at the Swettenham Arms for patrons only
Refreshments	Swettenham Arms. Tables outside
Pushchairs	Although the flat land would be ideal, the number of stiles makes the route impassable to pushchairs. Good flat paths can be found at the Brereton Heath Park

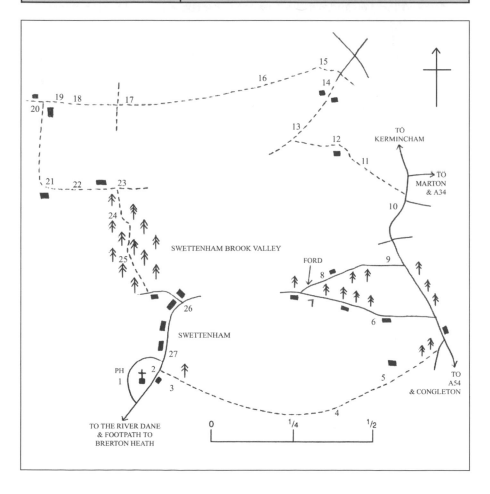

The Swettenham Arms is a picturesque building of whitewashed brick.
It has colourful hanging baskets and windows boxes, and seats outside
looking over the vast car park towards the church.

For a much longer route; ample parking and public toilets can be
found at Brereton Heath Park, just south of the A54 Congleton to
Holmes Chapel Road. From here it is a pleasant walk of 1½ miles to
Swettenham. Bear right from the car park, cross the main road and
take the bridleway opposite, leading past Davenport Hall. The path
crosses the River Dane and leads up to the village.

☺ Q: What hangs over the door of the village pub?
　 A: A lamp or lantern, which bears the pub's name: "Swettenham
　　　　　 Arms"

1. From the pub, head for the church and enter the churchyard
via the back gate.

☺ This is the church of St Peter. It originally had a wooden spire, but
　 this began to decay and several hundred years ago it was surrounded
　 by the present brick tower. The main church building was built in
　 stages throughout the years and has many unusual features, like the
　 different shaped windows on the far side and the "Gargoyles" or stone
　 faces which can be seen at many points.

　 Q: What type of animal can you find above one of the doors?
　 A: Over the side door is a horse's head in a gold crown

　 There are many yew trees around the small graveyard. They have thin,
　 dark green leaves and sometimes red berries. Can you recognise them?
　 They can often be found in graveyards because their wood was used
　 for making coffins. Yews can live to be thousands of years old.

　 Q: How many stone crosses can you see on the church roof?
　 A: Two, both on the southern side

2. Leave the church yard by the small gate at the front of the
church – the opposite side from the pub. Bear right onto the
lane and take the signed footpath almost immediately on the
left. Follow the fenced path between houses, then climb the
stile. Continue straight ahead across the open field.

☺ On the far horizon Shuttlingsloe, a hill in East Cheshire, one of the highest points in the county, can be seen over the treetops. It looks a bit like an upturned pudding basin.

3. **Cross the field and continue ahead, now with a fence/hedge on your left. At the end of the field cross the stile and continue ahead.**

☺ There may be crops growing in these fields. Grains, such as wheat or corn, or vegetables, especially potatoes. The farmer usually puts a different crop in each field every year, because each crop takes different nutrients out of the soil, and puts other nutrients back in.

   If there is wheat in the field you are walking through it may be planted with potatoes next year, and corn the year after, or it may be left as grass. See if you can recognise any crops you come across.

5. **Cross a further series of stiles, always keeping the fence/ hedge on your left.**

☺ Q: There are often cows in this field. Cows are females, so what are the males called?
   A: Bulls. Bulls often have horns and are usually much larger and heavier than cows. They are supposed to chase anything red. There is a saying "like red rag to a bull". In fact, bulls are not attracted to red at all.

☺ Take a look around and see if you can see what looks like a castle on the top of a hill in the distance. This is a famous Cheshire landmark - the castle of Mow Cop. It is actually a mock castle, or folly, just a tower and an archway, built as an attractive summerhouse. It can be seen from many places around the county.

5. **When the fence bears away to the left, continue straight ahead across the open field. On the other side of the field climb the stile to the left of the double gates. Continue ahead to the lane and bear left.**

☺ Nearby is the drive to Swettenham Hall, which at one time was the home of the rich lords who owned most of the area. They would rent farms and cottages to local people, who would then grow crops to try and earn their living.

6. **Keep with the lane for half a mile, passing several houses. After the old barn on the left, take the right turning, leading downhill.**

   Escape route: for the village centre or to return to the starting point do not turn off the lane, continue ahead.

7. **Follow the lane downhill beneath overhanging trees to Swettenham Brook.**

☺ This is Swettenham Brook. You can see the road goes through the stream. This is known as a "ford". There is a depth metre to show how deep the water is, in case it is too deep to drive across. How deep is the water today?

8. **Cross the footbridge and follow the lane uphill.**

Swettenham Brook ford

☺ Q: What is the name of the first farm on the left?
A: Brookhouse Farm

9. **At the top of the lane bear left, following another lane (for about a third of a mile). Beware of any traffic.**

☺ Q: What is the name of the village you are now entering?
A: Kermincham; there is a boundary sign on the left

Q: Notice the signpost on the right. How far is Swettenham Heath?
A: Three quarters of a mile

10. **Take the signed footpath on the left through the hawthorn hedge.**

☺ Again there may be cows in this field. You may also see rabbits running for cover as you approach, as there are many rabbit holes, or "burrows" hidden in the hedgerows.

11. **Pass behind the stables then take the stile on the right - bear diagonally left towards a further stile a short way ahead.**

☺ Q: Next to the house is an old barn. On the roof is a weather vane, which shows which way the wind is blowing. What type of animal is on the weather vane?
A: A horse

12. **Climb the stile onto the driveway in front of the house. Continue straight ahead, passing the barn on your left. Look out for the stile on the right – cross over this and bear left along the edge of the field. Climb a further stile, then continue straight ahead. Climb the next stile in the corner of the field and bear right along the driveway.**

Escape route: bear left along the driveway and follow it for half a mile, then bear left through a five bar gate into an area of woodland, and continue from Direction 23.

☺ There are hedgerows on both sides of the drive, made up of hawthorn bushes, blackberries, ferns and grasses and many other plants.

Hedgerows are very attractive and are usually colourful in every season. They give shelter for birds and small animals, and the red berries on hawthorn and holly bushes provide food through the cold winter months. Do not eat any wild berries yourself. Because animals eat them, it doesn't mean they are safe for people to eat.

13. **Pass "Cross Lane Cottage" on the right, then "Cross Lane Farm" on the left.**

☺ Q: What are the animals on the plaque at the gates to "Cross Lane Farm"?

   A: An owl and a hedgehog

14. **A short way after the farm go through the metal gate on the left and along the footpath**

☺ On the left there is an old bath for cows to drink out of. On the right you should be able to see houses in the village of Kermincham.

15. **Take the stile on the left and continue ahead with the line of trees on your left. Take the next stile and a further stile on the immediate left. Bear right along the edge of the field.**

☺ From here there are views for miles across the vast Cheshire Plain.

16. **Climb the next stile and keep straight ahead between the fenced paddocks. Cross over a soil bridle path and continue straight ahead, now with a hedge on your right.**

☺ For some of the way there are hawthorn hedgerows along the edges of the fields, and in some places just barbed wire fences. Many country hedgerows are hundreds of years old and were planted when England was a farming country, and each farm owned just a few fields. Today there are fewer farms, but they are usually larger with much more land.

   "Conservationists" are people who want to protect the countryside and make sure it is kept safe for us all to enjoy. They try to encourage farmers not to chop down hedges and trees. Most people agree that hedgerows look nicer than wire fences. What do you think?

   You may see horses grazing in the fields nearby. Also, if there are any crops growing, see if you can tell what they are.

17. Keep straight ahead at all times. At the "crossroads" of footpaths continue ahead.

Escape route: after about half a mile, you should pass a stile on the right. This point is a crossroads of footpaths. There is no sign to indicate as such, but there is a path leading off to the left along the edge of the field. For a short cut to Swettenham Village, follow the path which drops down to a rutted trackway. Bear right for a short way, then at the farm buildings go through a five bar gate on the left into an area of woodland. Continue from Direction 23.

18. Continue straight ahead towards farm buildings. A brick wall begins on your right.

☺ Look at the brick wall beside you. It is very old and the cement is flaking, making some of the bricks loose. Can you see the growths on the surface of the brick? This is called LICHEN and is a type of moss. On this wall there are several different types; yellow, green and white. Lichen needs very little water to survive. In hot weather it dries out, but will come back to life when it rains and it soaks up the water.

To the right the huge dish of the Jodrell Bank Radio Telescope can be seen. This is used for looking into space and tracking space ships.

19. Pass the stable and continue to the stile/gate. Keep straight ahead, passing the farm buildings and go through the five bar gate onto a driveway.

☺ Q: On the roof of the barn there is another weathervane. What animal is on it this time?
A: A cockerel, which is a male hen

The house ahead in the distance is Kermincham Hall. It is built of brick and has stone roof slabs. Like Swettenham Hall, which you passed earlier, the people at this Hall would have owned land in the area which they rented out to the locals.

Q: How many chimney pots can you count on the roof of the hall?
A: Nine altogether

20. Bear left along the driveway, passing the back of the barns.

☺ There may be tractors and other farm machines in these open barns. There are machines to plough fields, plant seeds, cut grass and even dig up potatoes. At one time all these things would have had to be done by hand.

21. **Follow the driveway as it leads to further farm buildings and bears around to the left. Continue ahead along the trackway.**

☺ Q: What is a young horse called?
   A: A foal

22. **At the next farmhouse go through the gate across the track and continue ahead.**

23. **At the next buildings bear right through a five bar gate, following the signed footpath downhill into an area of woodland.**

☺ Look out for squirrels running along the branches. There are two types of squirrel; red and grey. At one time there were more red squirrels but there are very few now. They find it more difficult to find food, while the grey squirrels are mischievous and very clever, and will raid bird tables and litter bins. If you see a squirrel it will almost certainly be a grey one.

24. **Follow the track downhill through the trees and cross the stream.**

☺ (AT THE BRIDGE) This is Swettenham Brook again. The trees in the meadows surrounding the brook are mainly alders and there is a great deal of wildlife here, particularly birds, including kingfishers and woodpeckers.

25. **After the bridge the track leads uphill. Bear left at the top.**

☺ Q: Look at the cottage on the right. Some of the windows have been bricked up. How many?
   A: Three on this side, and one on the front above the door

26. **Bear right onto the lane towards the centre of the village.**

☺ Q: What kind of flower is the cottage on the right named after?
(It has a round window upstairs and a face over the door)
A: A White Rose (White Rose Cottage)

27. Bear right at the war memorial before the church which takes you back to the Swettenham Arms.

Swettenham Checklist

☐	A CHURCH TOWER	☐	A HANGING LAMP
☐	A BLACK AND WHITE COW	☐	A HORSE
☐	A WHITE COTTAGE	☐	A TRACTOR
☐	A WOODEN BRIDGE	☐	A BRICK OR STONE BRIDGE
☐	A RABBIT'S BURROW	☐	AN OLD BATH
☐	A TELEPHONE BOX	☐	A POST BOX

26. Tatton Park

Tatton Park has something for all of the family. Impressive landscape, formal gardens, and no less than two historic halls in a setting with a rich ancient and medieval past. Of special interest to children: paddling and swimming are permitted in the lake, very popular on those rare hot summer days. There is a bathing enclosure on the eastern bank and a safe area marked by buoys. Close to the Hall there is a good childrens' playground. The Park is famous for its red and fallow deer and a host of other creatures, wild and domesticated, can often be seen.

For info: www.nationaltrust.org.uk then put Tatton in the search box. Tel: 01625 374435 (Infoline) or 01625 374400.

Starting point	Knutsford gates (SJ752792). There is a car park immediately on the right. The walk works equally as well from the main car park close to the Hall (SJ742817)
By rail	Nearest Station: Knutsford. A short walk through the town centre to the Knutsford gates of the park. Well signposted
Distance	4 miles
Terrain	Flat parkland, suitable for all weather
Maps	OS Landrangers 109 and 118 (Both needed to cover entire park)
Public Toilets	Tatton Mere car park Stableyard, near Hall
Refreshments	Stables Restaurant, near Hall Tuck Shop near Hall
Pushchairs	The flat park is ideal for pushchairs. The paths used are not concrete, so they are uneven, but easily negotiable

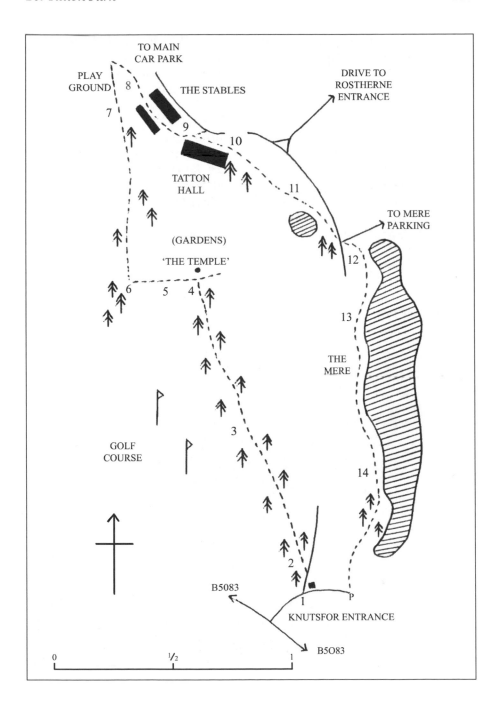

1. **From Knutsford follow the entrance driveway signed for Tatton Park. Go under the archway into the park itself. Go through the gate to the left of the cattle grid and continue ahead/left along a clear pathway between an avenue of oak and beech trees.**

☺   The park is now open to the public, but at one time it was private and belonged to the Lord of Tatton Manor. The family that lived at the manor were called the Egertons and were very wealthy and powerful. When the last Lord Egerton died he had no relatives to leave his land to, so he gave it to the National Trust. They look after the park and the house and open it to the public.

   These trees did not grow like this naturally in neat rows. The whole park has been carefully laid out, and in many places trees have been planted like this to form "avenues".

2. **Continue along the beech avenue, which soon runs alongside a golf course on your left.**

The stable block, Tatton Park

☺ The park has many deer, which can often be seen sheltering beneath the trees. There are two different types of deer here. Fallow deer are smaller and have white spots on their coats. Red deer are larger and have a reddish brown coat.

Q:	What do you think deer eat?
A:	Leaves and young shoots mainly, but also sometimes the bark of young trees

You may also see rabbits along the avenue. They live in holes in the ground called "burrows". You may see some burrows going down between the roots of the trees. Notice how the soil is very sandy, as much of the county of Cheshire is on top of sandstone.
(TOWARDS THE END OF THE AVENUE) Notice how some trees have fallen or been blown over and others have had to be cut down or "felled" for safety, so new trees have been planted to replace them.

3. Continue ahead at all times – taking care not to veer to the left at the end of the golf course. A clear, straight path continues ahead.

4. Eventually a folly "Temple" (a monument in the Hall gardens) should come into view straight ahead. Here bear left.

5. Follow the path to the metal kissing gate. Go through and continue ahead across the grassy field, bearing around to the right, heading for the far right corner of the field.

☺ There are often sheep grazing in this field. See if you can find any strands of wool in the grass, and keep a look out for deer or squirrels.

6. Go through the large metal gate and follow the trackway straight ahead through the trees. Continue straight ahead across the grass – with the fenced woods on your right – towards the children's playground.

7. Go through the gate to the left of the playground. Follow the trackway straight ahead. Bear right at the end of the playground along a pathway leading through trees. Bear right into the cobbled courtyard area, and bear left.

Here you will find toilets, baby changing, restaurant, tuck shop, gift shop, the entrance to the Hall and often a couple of Merry-Go-Rounds.

☺ (IN THE COBBLED STABLEYARD) The restaurant/building with the clock tower was once the stable block belonging to the hall, where up to fifty horses would have lived.
   (IN THE SHEDS OPPOSITE THE RESTAURANT) Here you can see Tatton's horse-drawn fire engine, with a row of firemen's helmets along its side. When it was in use it would have raced to put out any fire in the hall or the grounds.

Q: What colour is the fire engine?
A: Red

8. **Continue to the end of the stableyard. Go through the small archway after the Tuckshop then carefully cross over the cobbled driveway; take the path opposite through a gap in the holly hedge. Follow the path leading through the trees.**

Those wishing to visit the Hall should continue ahead along the cobbled drive. Hall opening times may vary due to special events.

9. **Go through the double iron gates and bear right, passing the front of the house.**

☺ This was the main entrance to the Hall. There are views from the windows along the avenue of trees and all over the parkland.

10. **Keep with the railings on your right, which bear around to the right after the Hall. When the path starts heading downhill, bear left to a wide grassy pathway crossing the open parkland, running approximately parallel to the Knutsford driveway. Soon the small mere should come into view on your right.**

☺ You may notice many planes passing overhead. There is usually one every few minutes. If you watch them carefully you can see them landing at Manchester Airport (large white buildings, just visible to the left, over the Cheshire Plain).

Merry-go-round, Tatton Park

During the war, Tatton Park was used for training people to use parachutes. They would jump out of a plane, open the parachute and then float down to the ground, landing safely in the wide open spaces in the park.

Keep a look out for the deer. In hot weather they like to shade beneath the trees.

11. Pass Melchett Mere on the right and continue a short way along the drive. Pass the turning to the left and continue to the gate crossing the driveway; do not go through, instead bear left across the grass towards the head of the lake.

12. Go through the metal kissing gate and continue ahead along the lakeside path.

☺ Tatton Mere is not a natural lake. It was made when the Monks from nearby Mobberley built a dam across a river, so the water rose and flooded the valley.

At the head of the mere is a sheltered part where birds can swim in safety. There are often Canada Geese with black and white heads, as well as swans and ducks.

13. **Keep with the path alongside the lake.**

   Route B: For an alternative route back to Knutsford bear left and keep close to the water's edge. On the other side of the lake pass the bathers' enclosure and continue through woodland to the large metal gate. Go through this and follow the driveway through the woods and bear right at the end for the town centre.

☺ In fine weather there are often boats and windsurfers on the water and sometimes people swimming. When it is very hot, cows often wade a short way out into the lake to have a drink and keep cool.
   (TOWARDS THE END OF THE LAKE YOU SHOULD PASS AN AREA OF TREES ON THE RIGHT) There are many squirrels in the woods around Tatton. If you are quiet you may see some. They eat nuts and seeds and can often be seen running along branches or rummaging around on the ground looking for food.

14. **Towards the end of the lake the path bears away from the hill, leading uphill and passing through the Knutsford gates car park. Continue ahead to the gates and entrance archway. Continue under the arch for Knutsford.**

Tatton Park Checklist

☐	A CHURCH TOWER	☐	A PLANE IN FLIGHT
☐	A SWAN	☐	A CANADA GOOSE
☐	A SQUIRREL	☐	A WHITE CAR
☐	A RABBIT	☐	AN OLD FIRE ENGINE
☐	A FALLOW DEER (small with white spots on coat)	☐	A RED DEER (larger, with a reddish brown coat)

27. Wharton's Lock and Shropshire Union Canal

The Shropshire Union Canal runs through this very picturesque area, providing a great deal of interest for children and adults alike. To add to the splendid scenery, the area is overlooked by the magnificent ruin of Beeston Castle, high up on its rocky crag.

This walk was originally intended as part of a much longer route, the rest of which had to be abandoned due to footpath problems (ie: they were blocked, kept disappearing, were unsigned, badly stiled etc etc). Nevertheless, this short circuit has been salvaged and retained, because this stretch of the canal is so spectacular. This is an ideal stroll for a warm summer's evening, before visiting the "Shady Oak" Pub, which overlooks the canal. (There are seats outside and also a childrens' playground.)

To completely avoid muddy fields and the road continue along the canal after Wharton's Lock and return the same way.

The Shropshire Union Canal

Starting point	Starting point: Bate's Mill Lane, near the Shady Oak Pub (SJ533603). There is parking at the Shady Oak for patrons. Also some places along the lane where the verge is wide enough for safe parking To find the Shady Oak, turn off into Tiverton village from the A49 just below Tarporley and follow the road. Take the first left turning, signed for Beeston Castle. The pub is half a mile on the left
Distance	Just under 2 miles
Terrain	Almost entirely flat; canal towpaths and public footpaths, and some stretches along lanes
Maps	OS Landranger 117
Public Toilets	No public toilets in the area. Toilets in the Shady Oak for patrons only. Nearest public toilets on Main Street, Tarporley
Refreshments	Shady Oak Pub
Pushchairs	The canal path is easily accessible for pushchairs. Walk from the Shady Oak along the towpath to Wharton's Lock, then return the same way

1. **From the Shady Oak cross the canal bridge and bear left, through the gate onto the towpath.**

☺ Canals are not rivers. They are man-made; dug out of the earth and filled with water. Many were built to carry goods, such as coal or in the case of Cheshire, salt from mines to factories. These goods are now carried by road or in some cases rail, and the canals are used mainly for pleasure. You will probably see several canal houseboats along this stretch of the water. These are called "narrow boats" and are often brightly painted and decorated with pictures of flowers. Some even have real flowers on them, in hanging baskets or in tubs on the roof. Many have names painted on them, like "Nutcracker" or "Shropshire Queen." See if you can see any with names.

Q: What number can you see on the bridge near the Shady Oak?
A: 109

2. Bear right along the towpath, with the canal on your right.

☺ (ON THE RIGHT) The castle is called Beeston Castle and it can be seen from many parts of Cheshire. The site has been used for defence for many thousands of years, but the castle we see today was built in

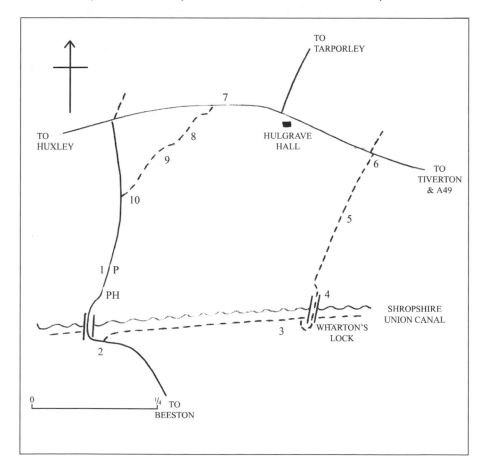

1220 by the Earl of Chester. Over the years it has been damaged in wars and is now in ruins, but still looks very impressive.

There are many plants along the edge of the water, including reeds, rushes, thistles and nettles. Have you noticed that the water is a sandy brown colour? This is because when the canal was dug, the sides and bottom were covered with a thick clay to make them water-tight, so the water would not just seep away into the ground. It is the clay which has coloured the water.

This is a popular place for the canal boats to stop for the night, mainly because of the pub. The people can meet each other and swap boating stories. It is also a popular place for swans and ducks, who know that they stand a chance of getting some food because there are so many people around. Swans, once they find a mate, stay together for life and take great care of their babies, or "cygnets" until they are nearly fully grown. Don't get too near the swans though, as they have quite a frightening hiss and can bite!

3. **Pass under the bridge, go up the steps and cross the canal by the footbridge. Take care, this water is deep!**

☺ This is Wharton's Lock. A "lock" is used as a kind of lift, to raise or lower canal boats. If you look at the level of the water on each side of the lock, you will see that one side is much higher than the other. If you are lucky you might be able to watch a boat using the lock, so you can properly see how it works.

The best chance of seeing the lock in use is at the week-end. There is a picnic site on the opposite side of the canal, close to the lock.

To avoid all roads continue along the canal, returning the same way.

4. **Take the metal kissing gate near the bridge and keep straight ahead across the farmed field – this is usually a well-trodden path.**

☺ This field may have cows in it, but it is often used for crops, such as wheat, which is a grass-like crop, or corn, which is very tall and green, and produces sweetcorn on "cobs" which you might recognise.

5. **Pass the small pond surrounded by hawthorn bushes on your right and continue ahead, soon with a hedge on your left.**

☺ The hedgerow on your left is made up of many different plants and trees, including hawthorn (with sharp thorns and bright red berries in the autumn and winter), sloe (again with sharp thorns and purple berries in the autumn) and oaks, which you have probably seen many times. A thick hedgerow like this is popular with birds and small animals as a shelter, so keep your eyes and ears open as you walk past.

6. **Cross the stile onto the lane and bear left. There is a narrow grass verge along the edge of the road.**

☺ Again there are views of the castle, over the hedges on the left. There is an old legend that says that King Richard II hid his treasure somewhere in the castle and that it is still there today. No-one has ever found it, and it is believed that if the treasure really exists, then it must be right down at the bottom of the well, which is very deep.

7. **Pass Hulgrave Hall on the left, then take the stile on the left. bear diagonally right across the field.**

   Alternatively, continue along the lane, taking the first left turning back to the Shady Oak.

☺ There are often cows in this field; you may be able to see their hoofprints in the mud. Even if there are no cows here at the moment, there may be cowpats on the ground, which tell you that there have been cows here recently! There are often brown flies on cowpats, which are called "dung flies". They eat the cowpat and lay their eggs in it.

8. **Climb a further stile, this time bearing diagonally left across the field.**

☺ Cows are quite curious and sometimes might come up to you, but will usually back away in fright if you make any sudden moves. If they come too close to you, just clap your hands. Never walk closely behind a cow, horse or any other large animal, in case you startle them and they kick out at you with their back legs.

9. Climb the next stile, bearing diagonally right.

☺ Q: What is the name for a young cow?
   A: A calf

If cows are lying down it is supposed to mean it is going to rain, but it isn't always true. Even the cows, like the weathermen, can make mistakes.

10. Climb the final stile onto the lane. Bear left, returning to the Shady Oak.

☺ There are hedges and trees along the lane, and sheltering in the undergrowth there might be rabbits, hedgehogs or field mice. There are often holes in the sandy soil, made by badgers, which have the sand piled up outside the entrance. Badgers only come out at night, so you are unlikely to see one. Sometimes foxes live in old badger holes, as it saves them digging a new home.

Moored boats near the Shady Oak pub

The hedges are mainly hawthorn, like you saw earlier. The trees along the lane are mainly oaks, which acorns come from. In the autumn you will probably see lots of acorns on the lane.

Q: What is the name of the pub next to the canal?
A: The Shady Oak. On the sign outside there is a picture of a large oak tree, with plenty of cool shade underneath its branches

The walk is over. Children to the play area. Adults to the bar.

Other places of interest

Beeston Castle
From the Shady Oak continue across the canal and follow the lane around to the left. The castle is well-signed.

Wharton's Lock Checklist

☐ A CANAL BOAT	☐ A SWAN
☐ A BRICK BRIDGE	☐ A CASTLE
☐ A COW	☐ A TRACTOR
☐ A BLUE CAR	☐ A BLACK AND WHITE HOUSE
☐ A RABBIT	☐ A HANGING PUB SIGN
☐ A DOG	☐ IVY

28. The Whitegate Way and Vale Royal

The Whitegate Way is a permitted footpath along an old railway line, passing through Vale Royal, and some of Cheshire's most attractive countryside. Relatively flat, and at many points there are views over the patchwork fields towards the Peckforton Hills.

Whitegate Way – white and wintery

☺ (AT WHITEGATE STATION) This was once a railway station. As you can see from the large concrete sign it was called "Whitegate" Station, after the village of Whitegate, which is close by. The house was once the ticket office and waiting room. It is now a private home.

1. **Bear right along the trackway, with the car park on your right.**

Starting point	Whitegate Way car park at the Old Station (SJ615679) well signed from A556 and A54 in the Vale Royal district
By rail	Nearest station: Cuddington, but there is a connecting bus service from Delamere Station
By bus	Services from Northwich, Middlewich, Delamere Station and Winsford
Distance	Entire route: 5 miles, with various escape routes
Terrain	Half of the route is along the Whitegate Way, an old railway track, now an attractive footpath. Also paths across farmed fields and trackways. All relatively flat
Maps	OS Landrangers 118
Public Toilets	Towards the end of the car park
Refreshments	Nowhere along the route, but try the cafe at Jardinerie Garden Centre, Cotebrook, or the Craft Centre on the A556 at Sandiway
Pushchairs	The Whitegate Way is ideal for pushchairs. The rest of the route, however, crosses farmland and is unsuitable. From the car park it is possible to walk for several miles in each direction along the old railway. Return the same way

☺ This track was once a railway line, and steam trains would have rattled along here. The railway was opened in 1870 to carry salt from the salt mines at Winsford to Cuddington, 6 miles away, where the salt could be loaded onto the main railway line that ran (and still runs) between Chester and Manchester.

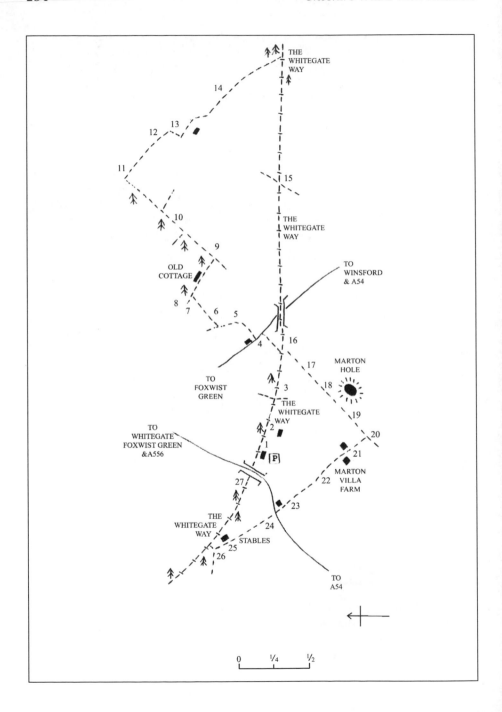

THE
WHITEGATE
WAY

14

13
12

11

10

9

OLD
COTTAGE

8
7   6   5

4

15

THE
WHITEGATE
WAY

TO
WINSFORD
& A54

16

17   MARTON
                      HOLE

TO
FOXWIST
GREEN

3

18

19

THE
WHITEGATE
WAY

2

1

20

TO
WHITEGATE
FOXWIST GREEN
&A556

P

21

MARTON
VILLA
FARM

22

27

23

THE
WHITEGATE
WAY

24

STABLES

25
26

TO
A54

0   ¼   ½

There are many silver birch trees growing along the track, which have narrow whitish trunks. There are also many nettles and brambles growing on the banks, so mind you don't get scratched or stung!

2. **Pass the toilet block on the right, continue ahead across the turning circle at the end of the car park and rejoin the Whitegate Way.**

☺ Amongst the other trees along the track there is a pear tree on the left. In the summer you should be able to see the fruit. The path is also used by horses, so keep a look out for the print of a horse's hoof on the ground.

The railway was in use for 82 years. It finally closed in 1952. In 1970 the metal tracks were lifted up and taken away to be re-used. When metal is heated under very great heat it melts and turns into a liquid, which can then be made into new objects.

3. **Avoid the first pair of footpaths to each side and continue ahead. At the next set of footpaths bear left, leading down a set of steps. Continue to the lane.**

☺ As you approach the lane keep a look out towards the left for a "thatched" cottage; thatch is a type of roofing made out of straw. The roof has to be replaced sometimes, by a craftsman called a "thatcher".

4. **Carefully cross the lane and take the stile almost opposite. Follow the narrow path through the woods. At the end of the woods climb the stile into the farmed field. Keep left along the edge of the field.**

☺ On the steep bank on the left there are many wild plants, some of which you may recognise. Gorse is a bush with very sharp prickles, which has yellow flowers throughout most of the year. Rosebay willow herb is a very common plant along hedgerows and on wasteland in the town. It is tall and has a lot of pink flowers at the top of its stem throughout the spring and summer.

5. **Follow the path as it begins to climb slightly and bears around to the left. At the top of the field cross the stile and bear right along the driveway.**

6. **At the end of the driveway bear right along a further driveway, signed for Gooseberry Hollow. Climb the stile at the end
   of the drive and continue ahead along the edge of the field.**

☺ Look back towards the railway line. Can you see how it runs along a bank
which has been built across the countryside? This is called an
"embankment". Have you ever noticed if you've been on a train that
the journey is always flat? Trains can't go uphill or downhill, so the
tracks are flat and embankments like this have to be built, or
"cuttings" are made through land that is higher. Trains also go over
bridges and through tunnels, all to keep the tracks level. You can see
two bridges from here. One goes over the road, the other over a farm
driveway.

7. **Follow the edge of the field, which begins to drop downhill to
   a stile.**

☺ Near the stile there is a damson tree. In the summer it will be covered
with dark purple fruit. Damsons are a type of plum and can be made
into jam or wine.

8. **Climb the stile and follow the footpath downhill through the
   woods.**

☺ You should soon pass the ruins of a row of brick cottages, with old
square windows and arched doorways. After the cottages the path goes
downhill between overhanging trees.

9. **Join the trackway at the bottom, bearing left.**

☺ In the woods on the left there is a stream flowing between the trees.
On the right is a high bank covered with ivy and bracken. Bracken is
a type of fern, with feather-like leaves. Ivy is a climbing plant. Can
you see how it has started to wind its way around the bark of the
trees?

10. **Avoid the first footpath to the left which crosses the stream
    – continue ahead along the track. As the track bears sharply
    to the right take the footpath that leads straight ahead
    through the woods, with the stream below. The path is**

narrow, but quite distinct and remains straight ahead above the stream.

☺ There are several willow trees along the stream. They like a lot of water, so they can often be found close to streams and ponds. There are also tall oak trees.

    Q: Do you know what the fruit of the oak tree is called?
    A: An acorn. The fruit of a plant contains the seeds. If you plant an acorn it will grow into an oak tree. Apples are fruit because they contain pips, which are the seeds of the apple tree.

11. At the end of the woods take the stile and bear right along the field, with a hedge on your right.

☺ The pond over on your left is private. There are often highland cattle in the fields in this area. They came originally from Scotland and have long horns and long shaggy coats, which would have kept them warm through the long Scottish winters.

12. Cross the next stile and bear right up a gravel trackway towards the whitewashed house.

13. After a short way – before the farmhouse – bear left across the stile, passing in front of the house. Continue ahead, crossing a number of stiles in close succession, until you come to a large open field. Here bear right, keeping close to the hedge.

☺ This is a very large field. At one time it would have been several smaller fields surrounded by hedges and trees, but over the years the farmers have chopped them down to make larger fields, so it is easier for their modern farming machines. Perhaps the field has a crop growing in it, such as potatoes or wheat. Can you recognise it?

14. At the end of the hedge keep straight ahead, cutting across the field towards the area of trees. Keep the trees on your right and continue to the metal kissing gate – this leads back to the whitegate way. Bear right.

☺ Back to the old railway again. At first there are views back over the countryside you have just walked through. Soon the track leads between bracken and overhanging trees and there are banks on both sides of the track, which means that this is a "cutting". Can you remember what that means? A "cutting" is a channel cut through the ground to make way for the railway.

15. **Avoid the first crossroads of footpaths and continue straight ahead. Eventually the track crosses over a road.**

☺ From here there are views over the first part of the walk. This part of the railway is higher than the surrounding countryside, so it is built on an "embankment".

16. **The track crosses over a driveway, soon after go down the steps on the left and to the metal kissing gate.**

Escape route: to return to the starting point, continue ahead along the old railway.

17. **Go through the metal kissing gate and bear right across the field. Go through a further kissing gate – here the direction signs are somewhat confusing and point straight ahead, but bear diagonally left across the field, heading gradually further away from the Whitegate Way, aiming for a cluster of trees across the flat field.**

☺ This field may have been planted with crops such as wheat or corn, or it may be grassy and have cows in it. The cows in Cheshire are usually black and white, a type called "friesians", but there are many different types of cow. You may have seen brown ones for example.

Whitegate Old Station sign

A cow can drink as much as 120 pints of water a day, which is about the same as a bathful each.

18. **You should come to Marton Hole on your left – fenced and with (recently planted) trees surrounding it. Bear right, with the fence and Marton Hole on your left.**

☺ You should soon come to a pond, with steep sides leading down to very deep water. This is called Marton Hole. It appeared overnight when the land fell into what was a hole left by salt mining. There are sometimes ducks or black coots on the water.

19. **Continue along the fence until you come to a five bar gate; here a metal kissing gate allows closer access to Marton Hole and the newly planted woods; avoid this and go through the five bar gate and follow the rutted farm track-way, with the hedge on your right. Avoid the immediate stile on the right.**

20. **The track opens into a large field. Continue ahead with the hedge and take the stile in the hedge on the right. Continue ahead, with the edge of the field on your left, heading towards the farm buildings.**

☺ From here are views over the Cheshire Plain. The hills in the distance are the Peckforton Hills, and there is a castle built there amongst the trees.

21. **Enter the rear of the farmyard – continue ahead for a short way but keep a look out for a stile on the left – climb this and keep straight ahead across a series of close stiles and finally through a gate into the yard in front of the farmhouse. Continue straight ahead along the driveway.**

☺ This is Marton Villa Farm. Further along the driveway there is a small reedy pond. In the summer there are waterlilies with round, rubbery leaves and red flowers. The lilies grow in the mud at the bottom of the pond, and the leaves and flowers grow up to the surface of the water on long stems. The flowers close at night and sometimes only open in good weather.

22. Cross the cattle grid, passing a small cottage on the left.

☺ On the left is a small cottage with roses growing on its walls. The bottom half of the cottage is made of local sandstone, and the top half is brick.

23. Keep ahead along the driveway, avoiding the driveways to the left.

☺ Q: Towards the end of the drive you should pass a bungalow on the right. A bungalow is a house which is all on ground level; it doesn't have an upstairs. What is the name of the bungalow?

A: "Calderstone"

24. Cross the lane and follow the trackway.

Escape route: bear right and follow the lane a short distance back to Whitegate Station, on the right.

25. Continue along the trackway, passing the stables on the right.

☺ Look out for blackberry plants along the sides of the track - they have long, prickly stems. The plant flowers in the spring, and in the summer the small berries can be seen, which will ripen from green, to red, and then to the familiar black. You should soon pass some stables on the right, so you have a good chance of seeing some horses, either at the stables, or along this trackway, which is used as a "bridleway"; which is a path for horses.

26. Take the footpath to the right immediately after the stables, which leads back to the Whitegate Way. Bear right.

☺ You may see rabbit holes in the banks along the track, so many rabbits live in the area. The trees along the old railway are also popular with small birds, such as sparrows and robins. There are more blackberry bushes, and also nettles and many wild flowers which attract insects like butterflies and dragonflies.

Soon you should pass under a road bridge. There are many more cars on the roads these days, and this bridge has had to have wooden supports put up underneath it, to help carry some of the extra weight.

27. Pass under the bridge and continue ahead to the car park.

☺ Just ahead is the old station building, which you passed at the start of the walk. The high wall on the right was once the platform where people would stand and wait for the trains. One of the downstairs windows of the house has a round pane of glass in it, which once held the station clock.

That's it. The end of the walk!

The Whitegate and Vale Royal Checklist

☐ A CHURCH STEEPLE		☐ A RABBIT HOLE	
☐ A BLACK AND WHITE COW		☐ A HORSE	
☐ IVY GROWING ON A TREE		☐ A POND	
☐ A PICNIC TABLE		☐ A BLACKBERRY BUSH	
☐ A WATER LILY		☐ A WHITE HORSE	
☐ A DOG		☐ METAL TRAIN TRACK	

29. Wincle

Wincle is on the south-eastern edge of the county. The River Dane just along the lane marks the boundary between Cheshire and Staffordshire. This is excellent hilly walking country, but quiet and unspoilt. The walk is short and if taken at a leisurely pace makes an enjoyable and varied half day out with some fine views into Staffordshire.

Starting point	Wincle (off the A54 Congleton to Buxton Road) (SJ964652). Parking available on the left of the road towards Danebridge
Distance	Entire route 2 miles To avoid the brief steep stretch at the beginning, park as close to the Ship Inn as possible and take the footpath just after the Inn. Keep straight ahead and then follow Direction 4 and onwards
Terrain	Good paths for most of the way. Uphill or flat on the way there, a pleasant downhill stroll on the way back
Maps	OS Landranger 118 OS Outdoor Leisure 24
Public Toilets	No public toilets
Refreshments	The Ship Inn, Wincle Beer garden at rear
Pushchairs	Not suitable for pushchairs due to the undulating land and the constant stiles

1. **Walk down the lane towards Danebridge and take the footpath on the left, almost opposite the telephone box.**

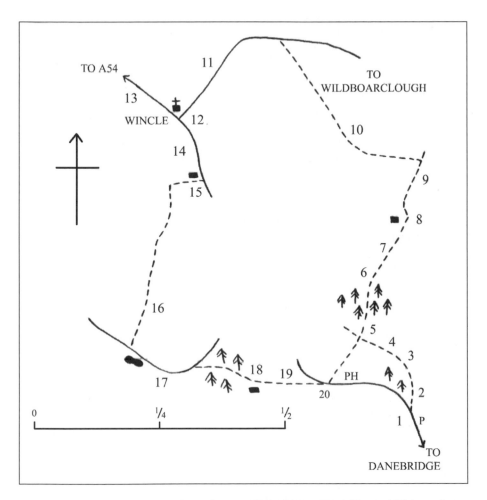

☺ Q: Notice the Post Box (TO THE RIGHT OF THE STILE) has the letters ER on it. What do you think they stand for?

A: They stand for Elizabeth Regina, which means Queen Elizabeth in Latin. This shows that this Post Box was made while the present queen was on the throne. Keep a look out for other post boxes near your home and see if they have any other letters, like GR (for King George) or VR (for Queen Victoria).

2. **Follow the footpath quite steeply uphill towards the left, climbing another stile.**

☺ Look at the tree stump. (TO THE RIGHT, SHORTLY AFTER THE STILE) Can you see how it is flaking away as it rots? One day, it will just turn back into soil and will feed the other plants that grow here.

3. **Continue uphill and climb a further stile under a row of trees.**

☺ These trees are Oaks, on which acorns grow. These are the seeds of the tree. They fall off in autumn and some of them will grow into new trees. If it is autumn or winter, see if you can see any acorns on the ground.

4. **Pass the back of some houses on the left, then keep straight ahead to the signpost – do not cross the stone stile over the wall at this point, instead bear right across the open field, passing a further signpost in the middle. Continue ahead, bearing downhill to a stile between conifers.**

☺ Keep an eye out for fircones on the ground. The cone carries the seeds of the tree. The seeds are much smaller than acorns and can blow in the wind to take root and grow elsewhere.

5. **Follow the path downhill through the woods.**

☺ New trees have been planted in the woods. They may have plastic "protectors" around their thin trunks, which stop wild animals from damaging them and eating their soft bark. The new trees on this side of the stream are mainly rowan, birch and lime. See if you can recognise them.

6. **Cross the stream by the wooden footbridge and continue up the path.**

☺ On this side of the stream there are more young trees, mainly oaks.

7. **Cross the stile and follow the path straight ahead, eventually leading towards a farmhouse.**

☺ (JUST BEFORE THE STILE INTO THE FARMYARD) Notice the water troughs for animals to drink out of. They are carved out of blocks of sandstone and are quite old. There are often cows or sheep in this field.

8. Climb the stone stile and bear to the right along the farm driveway.

☺ This is Bartomley Farm, and it too is built out of sandstone, a local stone, which can easily be cut into blocks for building. (TO THE RIGHT OF THE DRIVEWAY) This wall is also made of sandstone, but it is a different colour to the farmhouse, because it is weathered and dirty. If you take a close look at it, you can see why it gets its name; it is made up out of millions of grains of sand.

9. Follow the driveway as it swings to the left, leading uphill. (Keep with the lane, avoid the signed footpaths to the right.)

☺ (ON THE RIGHT) Look at the top of the hill. More sand. Much of the county of Cheshire has sand beneath it.

Look at the grassy bank by the roadside. There are many wild plants and grasses all growing together. In the spring and summer there are many different types of flowers. See how many you can spot.

Higher up there are good views to the left over the Wincle area.

10. The driveway soon levels out and Wincle church comes into view below on the left. At the end of the driveway bear left along the lane.

☺ (ON THE RIGHT, JUST BEFORE THE CHURCH) This is the local school, probably quite a lot smaller than your own school. Children from farms and villages several miles away come here to learn, because it is the only school in the area.

11. Climb the steps to the church.

☺ The church has a square tower with bells in it, which were rung on Sunday mornings to call the people to church. Some of the gravestones are very old. See which is the oldest you can find.

Q: Look at the metal things on each side of the church door. What do you think they are used for?

A: They are foot-scrapers, for cleaning mud and dirt off your shoes before going into the church.

12. **Leave the churchyard via the upper gate, to the left of the main church entrance.**

☺ The trees on each side of the gates are called yews. You can find them in many old churchyards. At one time people believed they would keep away evil spirits. The wood was also used to make coffins.

13. **Continue past the cottages on the right, then bear left along the lane leading downhill.**

☺ The cottages (ON THE RIGHT) are very old, and again are built of local sandstone with heavy stone slabs on the roof.

    Q: What is the name of the first cottage after the church?
    A: Little Chapter

14. **Continue along the lane, passing the church, then leading uphill.**

Wincle church

☺ Q: What is the name of the first farm on the right?
   A: Lane House Farm

(ON THE RIGHT, "THE PARSONAGE") This big house is "The
Parsonage", where the vicar of the church lived. (Parson is another
word for vicar.)

*Escape route: to return to the starting point continue ahead along
the lane.*

15. **Take the footpath on the right directly after The Parsonage.
Keep straight ahead, following the edge of the field. After the
row of hawthorn trees bear left, cutting diagonally across the
field. The stile is a few yards to the right of the telegraph pole
(it might be misleading to call it a stile at all – rather a few
pieces of wood tacked onto the end of a fence). Keep straight
ahead, keeping the fence on the left.**

☺ (SOME DISTANCE AHEAD THE PATH PASSES A STRANDED STONE
GATEPOST) This stone was once a gatepost. You can see the metal
hinge where a gate would have been hung, but it now stands alone in the
middle of the field and the wall in which it stood has now long since gone.

16. **Follow the track to the metal gate at the end of the field – the
gate on the right, not in the corner of the field. Go through and
bear left along the lane.**

☺ There is a pond opposite, with many different trees surrounding it and
bulrushes around its edges.

17. **Go over the cattlegrid and follow the lane. In a short way there
is a footpath off to the right. Bear diagonally left to another
stile – cross over into a woodland. Follow the path downhill.**

☺ These tall trees are called beeches. In the autumn you can find
beechnuts on the ground. They have prickly shells which split into four
pieces to let the seeds out. Some of the seeds will fall onto soil and will
begin to grow into new trees, others will be eaten by wild animals, such
as squirrels. If you are quiet you may see a squirrel collecting nuts or
running along the branches above.

18. At the bottom of the woods climb over the stone stile, taking care as it may be slippery on the other side. Continue ahead along the edge of the field, passing a farmhouse on the right. Climb the stile and cross the farm driveway, climbing the stile opposite.

☺ There may be horses in this field. There is a small stable in the (LEFT) corner.

19. Cut across the field to another stile and steps that lead down to the lane. Bear right, passing the Ship Inn. (There is a beer garden at the back of the Inn, very pleasant on a sunny day.)

☺ Q: What is painted on the hanging sign over the door of the inn?
    A: A ship, of course! What else would you expect to find at the Ship Inn!

20. Continue along the lane, heading downhill to the parking spaces.

☺ Q: What is the name of the first house on the left after the inn?
    A: Lilac Cottage

Take care on the road. Be aware of oncoming traffic.

Wincle Checklist

☐ IVY ON A TREE OR GATEPOST	☐ A BLACK AND WHITE COW
☐ AN OLD FASHIONED LAMP POST	☐ A HORSESHOE
☐ A HANGING INN SIGN	☐ A SANDSTONE WALL
☐ A SHEEP	☐ A BIRD'S FEATHER
☐ A GRAVESTONE	☐ A CHIMNEY

30. Windgather Rocks

This area is a complete contrast to the more typical flat farmland generally associated with Cheshire. It is wild and rugged in parts, dramatic, exciting and ... windy.

For a really long walk the Shining Tor route can be added to the end of this.

Starting point	**Pym Chair car park (SJ995768) from Macclesfield follow signs for Buxton, then Goyt Valley. Pass Jenkin Chapel on the corner at Saltersford, follow the road uphill, then bear left before the descent into the Goyt Valley. The car park is on the right**
By bus	**Services from Macclesfield to Kettleshulme**
Distance	**4 miles, with various escape routes**
Terrain	**Moorland paths and farm trackways Some uphill stretches**
Maps	**OS Landranger 118 OS Outdoor Leisure 24**
Public Toilets	**None along the route. The nearest are in the Goyt Valley, across the dam, or the car park and picnic area at Lamaload Reservoir**
Refreshments	**Nearest place is the Tea Cosy Cafe, on the main road in Kettleshulme, open Friday to Monday. Closed in January**
Pushchairs	**Not suitable at all**

☺ (AT THE CAR PARK) This place is called Pym Chair, supposedly after a man called Pym, who may have been a highwayman – a man who robbed passers-by at gunpoint, or a preacher; no one is really sure which.

1. **From the main Pym Chair car park face the road and bear right across the grass verge at the side of the lane. After a short distance there is a stile on the right. Cross this and bear left along the drystone wall.**

☺ This is one of the windiest and loneliest parts of Cheshire. In fact, you are right on the boundary between Cheshire and Derbyshire, and this type of countryside is more typical of Derbyshire. If you have been on other walks in Cheshire you will know that it is mainly flat with green fields, woodlands and colourful hedgerows, but here the land is higher, and to your left you should be able to see over the hills towards the lower parts of the county.

Ahead there are views of the Goyt Forest, in Derbyshire. The trees are mainly conifers, which have their seeds in cones, like a fir cone or a pine cone which you have probably seen many times. Conifers usually have long, dark green needles instead of leaves; they have very straight trunks and they grow fairly quickly, so they are often grown for their wood.

Q: Most (but not all) conifers are "evergreens". Do you know what an "evergreen" is?

A: It is a tree or bush which does not lose its leaves in the winter, so it stays green all the year round. Many evergreen trees and bushes are used as decorations at Christmas, like Christmas trees, of course, and also holly and ivy.

If it is autumn or winter, if you look towards the forest you should see that some of the conifers have changed colour, and have gone brown or yellow and may have started to lose their needles. These trees are "larches" and they are grown for their wood. They are obviously not evergreens, but "deciduous".

Q: This is an easy one. Do you know what it means if a tree is "deciduous"?

A: Even if you don't know, you can probably guess. Deciduous trees lose their leaves in the winter. The tree goes to sleep for the

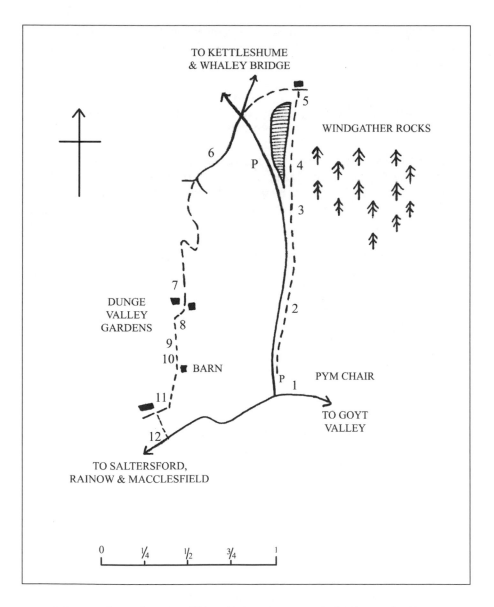

winter, and new leaves will begin to appear again in the springtime.

This type of countryside is called "moorland". Apart from the forest, which was planted by man, there are very few trees. There are wild grasses and low bushes, like heather, which grows well in places like this, where it can be bitterly cold in the winter, and very windy, even on a summer's day. Heather has small colourful flowers of white, pink, purple or red. It is often used in gardens as part of a rockery or flowerbed.

2. **Keep ahead, following the wall. Avoid the stile on the left, which just leads back to the lane.**

☺ On the right there is a conifer plantation, which is like a small forest. The ground between the trees is covered with dead needles, which have fallen from the trees. Evergreens shed their leaves gradually throughout the whole year, and new ones grow all the time, so they are never without leaves.

3. **Pass the plantation on the right, go through the gate and continue ahead along the top of Windgather Rocks, taking care of the drop on the left over the edge of the rocks.**

☺ This is Windgather Rocks, and you can probably tell how they get their name. It is high up here and often very windy. If it is windy, don't go too near the "cliff edge" or you might find yourself getting blown off! The "cliff" is popular with rock climbers, who come to practise here. They can often be seen climbing the rocks at the weekends.

4. **Continue straight ahead, go through the gate – avoiding the gate to the right leading down into the forest. Keep ahead along the top of the rocks at all times, until a drystone wall starts on your left.**

☺ The Goyt Forest should be downhill on your right. As you can see, the trees are mainly conifers. Sometimes areas of the trees are cut down and the wood is taken away to be made into furniture, or "woodpulp", from which paper is made. New trees are then replanted, so there will always be trees here.

5. **At the end of the field go through a stone gateway onto a gravel track in front of a farmhouse. Bear left and follow the driveway, avoiding the stile to the right. Keep with the driveway, then bear left onto the lane. At the crossroads go straight across.**

Escape route: at the crossroads bear left, which will return you to the starting point in just over a mile.

☺ This lane has a "T" sign at the start, which means it is a dead end – it doesn't lead anywhere. There are often sheep or cows in these fields around you. Sometimes they lie close to the walls, keeping out of the wind, and who can blame them? Down below, flowing through the middle of the valley there is a stream called Todd Brook, which empties into a reservoir, which was made by building a dam, or large wall across the valley, so the valley became flooded. It is called Toddbrook Reservoir, and it is a few miles away at Whaley Bridge.

6. **Avoid all footpaths, keep with the lane, leading downhill. At the end of the lane there are several driveways – keep ahead over the cattle grid or over the stile to its side. Continue ahead. Avoid tracks to either side, keep with the main drive, crossing a stream and bending sharply to the right.**

☺ There are views from here over fields which probably have grazing cows and sheep in them. There are gorse bushes along the driveway, with their prickles and yellow flowers; sometimes the flowers smell of coconut. Soon the drive crosses a stream.

   Notice how there are many trees growing close to the water, including colourful rowans. Here there is some shelter for them from the wind, and also plenty of water for their roots. There are many trees along this trackway - some are conifers and some are broad-leaved trees. Can you tell which are which? Broad leaved trees include sycamore, oak and horse chestnut.

   Sycamore trees have clusters of "keys" or "helicopters" in the autumn, which are the tree's seeds. When they fall down they are blown away by the wind, sometimes quite far away. This is so that a new trees will not begin to grow near the old one. Oak trees produce acorns which are their seeds. In the spring, horse chestnut trees have lots of flowers, usually white, which look like candles. Conkers come from horse chestnut trees. The conker is the seed of the tree, and if you plant one it should grow into a small tree. If it is late summer or autumn see if you can find a sycamore key, an acorn and a conker.

7. **Go through the gate of Dunge Valley Farm, continue ahead with the driveway, passing the main farmhouse on the left.**

Dunge Farm Gardens are open to the public throughout the summer. There is a "no dogs" sign at the farm gates. This refers to visitors to the gardens, not users of the public footpath. Keep to the public right of way when passing through the gardens and keep your dog on a lead.

☺ **Q:**   You should pass the farmhouse on the left. What is the date on the plaque on the front?

A: 1749

The path now passes through the gardens of Dunge Farm, where there are many colourful plants and trees, which grow well in this sheltered spot. Look out for roses and wild dog roses.

8. **Cut across the small gravel car park to a signed footpath on the opposite side, leading through an area of trees and shrubs, following the grassy path, signed intermittently. Keep ahead on the main path and cross the stream by the plank bridge.**

Windgather Rocks

☺ Along the stream there are large stones covered with moss, and also some fallen logs, also covered with moss and other small, moisture loving plants. The logs, even though they are dead, provide a home for many insects and plants. There are also many blackberry bushes and ferns.

9. **Follow the path uphill to the stile. Keep left to a further stile. Keep straight ahead. At first there is a fence on the right. (Negotiate the marshy area as best you can – basically keep ahead, uphill alongside the stream.)**

☺ Parts of this field are covered with marsh; a water-logged area. Can you see the tall green grass with very pointed ends? This is marram grass. It can often be seen growing where it is wet, or at the seaside in sandhills.

10. **Keep straight ahead. Soon a barn should come into view – head for this. Pass the barn and continue ahead, crossing the stile in the fence. Follow the path ahead, keeping the fence on your left.**

☺ Q: After a short way a rooftop should come into view straight ahead. How many chimneys does it have?

  A: Two, one at each end of the main roof. This is called Green Stack. It is quite a remote house and will easily get snowed in after a heavy snowfall.

11. **Keep left with the drystone wall. Follow the path downhill to a stile on the left of the house. Continue downhill and join the driveway. Almost in front of the main house bear left and cross the stream (there is sign indicating the crossing place). Head uphill, with your back to the house. There should be a clear pathway leading straight up across the middle of the field.**

☺ There are often sheep in this field. Sheep are hardy animals and can live in the strong winds and cold conditions that are common here. Most sheep in this area are white, but occasionally you see a black one – see if you can spot any. There are about 1,000 million sheep in the world. In New Zealand there are twenty times more sheep than people!

12. **At the top of the field cross the ladder stile over a drystone wall. Continue ahead to join the lane. Bear left along the lane, keep well in. The lane leads uphill to Pym Chair car park.**

☺ You should pass a house on your left. Can you imagine what it would be like to live here? The winters here can be very long and cold and it is quite common for there to be deep snow; it is also quite common for these lonely houses to be snowed in for days. Imagine that, not being able to go to school until the snow melted! This is the very last part of the walk and it is quite steep; at the top of this road is the car park at Pym Chair where the walk started. Try going slowly uphill and counting your footsteps.

Windgather Rocks Checklist

☐	HEATHER	☐	A ROCK CLIMBER
☐	AN EVERGREEN TREE	☐	A SHEEP
☐	A WHITE HOUSE	☐	A HORSE
☐	A FIRCONE	☐	A COW
☐	A STONE RUIN	☐	A CONKER/HORSE CHESTNUT TREE

50 Questions and Answers for boring journeys

Some are as easy as falling off a log. Some are much harder. Most are mentioned in the text of the book. The answers are at the end of the section.

Cheshire

1. What is the capital city of the county of Cheshire?

2. Lewis Carroll, who wrote "Alice in Wonderland" lived at Daresbury in Cheshire. Which animal character in his stories had a connection with Cheshire?

3. Chester was at one time a fort, but who built it?

    A: The Greeks
    B: The Romans
    C: The Chinese

4. Where in Cheshire can you see a working mill that makes cotton, and a giant waterwheel?

5. There was much fighting in Cheshire during the Civil War. The government were one side in the war. Do you know who they were fighting?

6. The Cheshire childrens' writer, Alan Garner, has set many of his books in the county. Do you know where his most popular book, "The Weirdstone of Brisinghamen" is set?

7. Do you know which large Cheshire hall has been used in many television programmes, including "Red Dwarf" and "Neighbours"?

8. What two types of deer are found in Cheshire parkland?

9. In which Cheshire village might you find a stone elephant?

10. Whose face is carved over the well at Alderley Edge?

11. Bread is made from which crop that is grown in many places in Cheshire?

12. Do you know what "dialect" is?

See if you can guess what the following local Cheshire words mean:

13. FLECK - does it mean:

    A: A flea
    B: A small stream
    C: A female horse

14. AGGED - does it mean:

    A: Angry
    B: Shy
    C: Tired

15. COBNOBBLE - does it mean:

    A: To tell off
    B: To win at a game
    C: A type of biscuit

16. SKEW-WIF or SKEW-WIFTER - does it mean:

    A: A type of hat
    B: Bent, or not straight
    C: A type of stew

17. ADDLE - does it mean:

    A: Lazy
    B: To earn money
    C: To argue

18. In which Cheshire castle have episodes of "Doctor Who" and "Sherlock Holmes" been filmed?

19. The names of several Cheshire towns end in "wich". This means they are salt mining towns. Can you name any?

20. What space-age piece of equipment would you expect to see at Jodrell Bank?

Nature

21. What is the fruit of the oak tree called?

22. Which birds are known for stealing shiny objects?

23. From which tree do conkers come?

24. Which prickly plant with red berries is often used in decorations at Christmas?

25. What is a Red Admiral?

26. What type of animal is a Red Setter?

27. What is a baby duck called?

28. That was easy, but do you know what a baby swan is called?

29. What is a rabbit's home called?

30. Some birds "migrate" in winter. What does this mean?

31. What is a deciduous tree?

32. How does a horse "groom" itself?

33. How many "toes" does a cow have?

34. Some animals, like hedgehogs, "hibernate" in the winter. What does that mean?

35. Which small bird is famous for its red chest?

General Knowledge

36. Can you name the four points of the compass?

37. Which way does the needle on a compass always point?

38. What is the name of the Queen's famous London home?

39. Which childrens' programme has got a colour and a boy's name in the title?

40. Do you know what glass is made from? (There is a lot of it near the sea.)

41. What colour do you get by mixing yellow and blue paint?

42. In Britain, do cars drive on the right or the left of the road?

43. What type of book has the meaning of words in it?

44. In which country do the men traditionally wear kilts?

45. How many sides are there to a rectangle?

46. What is the name of the Queen's eldest son?

47. Do you know what the capital of France is?

48. How many pennies are there in a pound?

49. How many 5 pences are there in a pound?

50. How many numbers are there on a telephone?

Answers

1. Chester
2. The Cheshire Cat
3. B - The Romans
4. Quarry Bank Mill, Styal
5. The King, Charles I
6. Alderley Edge
7. Lyme Hall
8. RED and fallow deer are the most common
9. Peckforton
10. The Wizard of Alderley
11. Wheat, though bread can be made of other grains as well
12. It is a local way of speaking
13. A - A Flea
14. C - Tired
15. A - To tell off
16. B - Bent, not straight
17. B - To earn
18. Peckforton Castle
19. Northwich, Middlewich and Nantwich
20. The huge white dish of the radio telescope
21. An acorn
22. Magpies
23. Horse Chestnut
24. Holly
25. A butterfly
26. A dog
27. A duckling
28. A cygnet
29. A burrow or warren
30. They fly south to warmer countries

31. It loses its leaves in winter
32. By rolling over
33. Two, or rather each hoof is split in two
34. They go to sleep until the spring
35. A Robin, or Robin Red Breast
36. North, south, east and west
37. North
38. Buckingham Palace
39. Blue Peter
40. Sand
41. Green
42. Left
43. A dictionary
44. Scotland
45. Four
46. Prince Charles
47. Paris
48. One hundred
49. Twenty
50. Ten

Some games ideas for long journeys

1. If you are in a car, you will undoubtably pass many road signs.
   Children can have about eight secondsworth of fun guessing
   what each sign means, and might also retain some helpful
   knowledge for later in life.

2. Think of a subject eg: animals, birds, trees, and each child or
   member of the party has to say a type of animal. After a few
   rounds, it will get more difficult. If you can't answer you are out.
   The winner, obviously, is the one remaining at the end.

3. I-Spy, an old favourite.

4. Guess who? Think of a famous person, cartoon character etc
   and the children have to guess who it is by asking questions,
   such as: are you a woman? Are you on television? Give them the
   odd clue occasionally to help them along.

5. Counting things. On a car journey, the most obvious subject
   would be cars. Each person picks a different coloured car, the
   winner is the one who has pointed out the most at the end of the
   journey.

Also from Sigma Leisure:

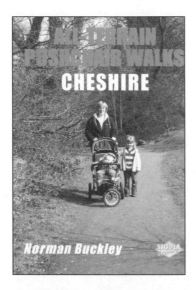

All-Terrain Pushchair Walks
Cheshire
Norman Buckley

30 graded walks, from level routes around pretty Cheshire villages to more adventurous hikes across the hillsides. Detailed directions and a map are provided for each route, together with some stunning photographs.
£7.95

Best Tea Shop Walks in Cheshire
Clive Price

"... A winning blend of scenic strolls and tasty tea shops." – Cheshire Life.

First published in August 1995 and subsequently updated with major revisions due to some tea shop closures and consequent re-routing of walks.
£7.95

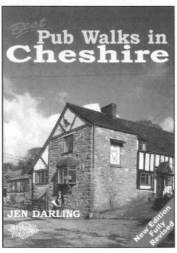

Best Pub Walks in Cheshire 2nd Edition
Jen Darling

This is the second edition of a guidebook to the walks and pubs of Cheshire.

"I was delighted to be asked to put a few words on paper ... this book brings together a series of suggestions for your enjoyment."
– John Ellis, Cheshire Tourism
£7.95

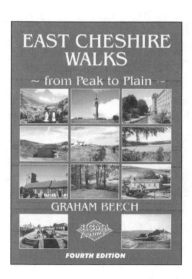

East Cheshire Walks
from Peak to Plain 4th Edition
Graham Beech

The definitive guide to walking in East Cheshire is now in its fourth edition! Completely updated and revised, with nearly 40 walks covering 250 miles, there really is something for everyone. Footpath diversions fully documented.

£7.95

50 Best Cycle Rides in Cheshire
Edited by Graham Beech

"Every cyclist should be leaping into their saddles with this new book."
– The Cheshire Magazine.
Completely updated

£8.95

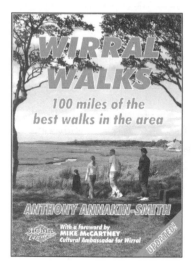

Wirral Walks 2nd Edition
100 miles of the best walks in the area
Anthony Annakin-Smith

A completely revised and updated edition of this popular collection of 25 walks from around 2 to 10 miles, covering a total of 100 miles through the best of the local landscape. The author's careful research highlights the interesting and unusual features seen along each route.

£8.99
New edition available in 2010

Discovering Manchester
2nd Edition
Barry Worthington

This stylish walking guide doubles as a detailed account of the city's architecture, its history and tourism attractions. There are walks throughout Manchester including such major entertainment and cultural centres as the Bridgewater Hall, Urbis, the Museum of Science and Industry, the Lowry and many more. Explore the entire city – from the Corn Exchange to G-Mex, from the Cathedral to Affleck's Palace.

9.99

Available May 2010

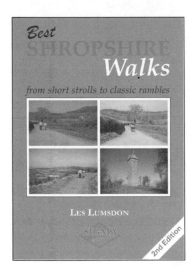

Best Shropshire Walks 2nd Edition
From short strolls to classic rambles
Les Lumsdon

A new revised edition of this much loved guide contains 36 walks, including 12 completely new routes, located in all parts of the county. Several walks feature fine hill walking on the Welsh borders and others start from delightful villages and hamlets in the north and east of the county.

£8.99

Available February 2010